Alex Williams was born in 1957 in Melbourne, Australia. He had an unsurprising upbringing in the suburbs, living the standard Australian dream. At the age of 17, all of that changed when he was diagnosed with Type 1 Diabetes. Since then, he has lived in Brisbane, Saudi Arabia and India, working with the massive computers that power the financial world.

For my wife, Donna, without whose (almost) endless support
this could not have happened.

Alex Williams

MARATHON DES SABLES –
A TYPE 1 DIABETES
ADVENTURE

AUSTIN MACAULEY PUBLISHERS™

LONDON • CAMBRIDGE • NEW YORK • SHARJAH

A CIP catalogue record for this title is available from the British Library.

ISBN 9781035859764 (Paperback)
ISBN 9781035859771 (ePub e-book)

www.austinmacauley.com

First Published 2024
Austin Macauley Publishers Ltd®
1 Canada Square
Canary Wharf
London
E14 5AA

Table of Contents

Prologue 1974

It was August 1974 and my mother, two younger brothers and I had been living in The Basin since before winter had started. This was the first house my mother had found to rent since we had needed to move away from the family home. My parents had split and, being in the 70s, my newly single mother was finding it difficult finding a landlord who would trust her to pay the rent. Today we think back to the 70s with a warm, cosy feeling of nostalgia for a world more innocent and burnt orange kitchens. But for a single woman with young children, it could be, and was, a tough place.

The Basin sits at the base of The Dandenongs, the iconic collection of hills to the east of Melbourne. If you wanted to find somewhere that suffered all of the hardships associated with winter in Melbourne, you couldn't go much past The Basin. From late April until early September, The Basin was cold, wet and miserable. Sure it held an idyllic charm, almost a faux Swiss/European quaintness, but during those months the 'Swiss quaint' was difficult to identify.

As I was now in my final year of high school which, in Australia, was the year when your final exam results dictated if you could go to university or not, and therefore your future direction in life, moving schools was not even discussed, let alone considered. It went without saying that I would need to make the daily journey from The Basin to Mitcham, where my high school for the past five and a half years was. This involved either catching a bus to the nearest station, or walking the three kilometres, then catching the suburban train to Mitcham, then walking another one and a half kilometres to the school. At the end of the day, the reverse journey was required, of course. So on any given day of the week, I could find myself walking for up to nine kilometres, often in the dark, through rain and hail and icy wind, to and from school.

Add to this picture the underlying emotional upheaval of having your family gradually fall apart and for a 17-year-old, something was bound to give.

The Young Diabetic in Cubicle 3

"Yes doctor, the young diabetic in Cubicle 3," said the nurse as she talked with one of the doctors in the emergency ward of Box Hill Hospital. My mother and I weren't silly; we knew which cubicle we were sitting in.

This was how I found out that my life, my world, and my existence had changed forever. There was no going back from this moment.

All my mother and I knew about diabetes up to that point was the same as most people back then, and to this day, and that is that it involved injections, lots of them. With just the two of us huddled away in the cubicle, the news that came drifting over the partition left me shell-shocked. My mother, with all of the upheavals and dramas that she had endured over the years, especially over the last 12 months as a single mother of three boys, had learnt to grit her teeth and take the slap as she had so many times before. But for me, a 17-year-old teenager, this was a shock too far. I burst into tears.

After what seemed like an eternity, the doctor came sweeping in with his entourage in tow. His white coat was open and ballooning at the back. His entourage included a junior doctor, a student doctor and a nurse, all of whom had clip boards in the crook of their arm. The nurse was frantically writing down instructions; the student was scribbling notes desperately and the junior doctor was reading aloud from his clipboard. Even though we'd only spoken with the receptionist as we entered the hospital and the nurse as she took some blood from my arm earlier, I had apparently already built up a medical history that stretched across a number of pages.

Being in the 70s, doctors were still considered by most people to be demi-gods, beyond being questioned. They were the ones with the years of university and experience, so their word was beyond us mere mortals. My mother and I sat there as they all talked amongst themselves, almost as if we weren't even there. The nurse took notes, the student doctor remained silent and in the background, except to acknowledge that he had made note of the latest pearl of wisdom from the senior doctor, and the junior doctor quietly read information aloud from his clipboard, answering the senior doctor's clipped queries.

Suddenly, with virtually no warning, the senior doctor turned his ray of wisdom in our direction. His tone softened a little as he spoke to my mother. He explained in a couple of brief sentences, all the while holding a tone that portrayed that he actually expected my mother to understand everything that he was saying, that I was a very sick lad and that she should have brought me to the hospital sooner. Working on the assumption that my mother was already quite well acquainted with diabetes, he explained in his clipped manner that I would be in hospital for about a week, then having injections for the rest of my life. I would need to follow a strict diet and that, so long as I followed the rules without deviation, I should be able to live relatively well for close to a normal time frame. I would learn the basics of living with 'juvenile diabetes' during my week in hospital. Other doctors and nurses would answer any further questions we had.

Only then did he turn to me.

"Well, my friend, you have been a very sick fellow, but we're here to help you get better." I sat there with my eyes red and puffy from my tears, desperately trying to keep myself under control. Crying in front of this important person was to be avoided, or so I told myself.

"What you have is called Juvenile Onset Diabetes and it's when your pancreas isn't making insulin. It is a serious illness, but one that we can manage."

"How long will I need to have injections for?" I blurted out. "I don't like injections."

"Well, that's something that we will teach you about. You will need to have injections for the rest of your life, but you will learn to get used to them."

I felt totally gutted. Only this morning I had left home as normal to go to school, but with instructions from my mother to go to see the family doctor on the way home. And now here I was in the emergency ward of a hospital being told that my life had changed forever. How could this all be happening?

As I sat there with my mother, both of us feeling overwhelmed, little did we realise just how radically my life really had changed. In the space of 15 minutes, I had gone from being a typical, if a little bit sickly, 17-year-old, to being a member of an elite group of humans comprising roughly 0.5% of humanity who were living with this chronic illness. So long as I learnt all of the rules and took my insulin and ate the right foods at the right times, I could hope to live almost as long as my friends. But if I didn't learn the rules, or chose not to stick to them closely, I could expect any number of a group of horrible complications that came with the diagnosis.

All I could think as we both sat there in a daze was: "Fifteen minutes ago, I was normal. Why me?"

Thirty Four Thousand Injections Later, Give or Take – 2008

Jump forward 34 years, six or seven ambulance trips to hospital, countless episodes of low sugar, known as 'hypos', and roughly 34,000 injections of insulin. It's April 2008 and I was on the train home from my day at work in the city. Along with half the people on the crowded train, I was reading a copy of the daily commuter newspaper handed out at the station.

There were the usual stories about local celebrities, politicians doing silly things, the latest out-of-reach model from Mercedes. I moved on through the letters pages, where young, spotty-faced, love-sick commuters write anonymous notes to the pretty girl they saw the previous day. It was all mildly amusing, but in a humdrum sort of way. I was about to give up on the paper when I turned the page for the final time and something grabbed my eye. Having lived in Saudi Arabia for five years and spent many hours driving and walking through the desert, my eye was tuned to look for anything that might be about Saudi, the Middle East or the desert. And what I was looking at now was a half-page story with a photo of a person dressed in shorts and running shoes and a desert hat apparently running through the desert. Intriguingly, the person also had on what appeared to be a backpack.

As I sat on the crowded suburban train, squeezed into my seat and with my bag tucked between my feet on the floor, the story was telling me about another world. This was the world of extreme duration events and specifically the Marathon Des Sables. I'd heard about this event, and that it was some sort of crazy race across the desert carrying all of your stuff on your back. But that was about the extent of my knowledge. The story I was now reading, though brief and without many details, was setting my mental wheels in motion. I learnt from the story that the name 'Marathon Des Sables' is French, and means 'Marathon of the Sands'. The event was started many years ago by a French adventurer called Patrick Bauer, after he had undergone an experience in the Sahara desert in Morocco.

The event entailed the competitors covering a distance of about 240 kilometres in stages, set over a seven-day period. Each competitor carried all of their gear and food requirements, with water being supplied to them along the way. And the reason why the story was in the newspaper at all was because the 2008 running was about to start.

Even though the story held only scant information about the Marathon Des Sables, it set my mind running, and for the rest of the hour-long trip home, I could think of little else. I even sent my wife Donna a message, telling her that I had something to ask her when I got home. My mind was churning; my excitement was up. Could it be possible that I would again experience the magic that is the desert at night?

The Magic Kingdom Calling – 1995

Saudi Arabia—sigh.

Thanks to 'The recession we had to have' in Australia around 1993, a quote from our then Prime Minister Paul Keating, I must have been one of the last people in Australia to be retrenched.

Seven years previously, my family and I had moved from Melbourne to Brisbane with the hope of providing our growing family with a brighter future. Melbourne and Victoria had been struggling through a serious economic downturn for a number of years and, when a good job was offered to me in Brisbane, Donna and I decided it was an opportunity too good to pass up for a change to our family life. Besides, most of Donna's close family was now living in the Brisbane area after moving over from New Zealand, so it was also a chance for her to be closer to them. After moving to Melbourne five years previously, Donna was missing her family.

It all seemed to come together in a neatly serendipitous manner.

Life was good. Sure, interest rates were going up and the mortgage payments were getting bigger, but I had a good job and Brisbane had a care-free atmosphere that matched its seemingly limitless sunshine.

The company I was with was going through a large growth period and was in the process of buying up smaller companies who were struggling with the crippling interest rates. You would think that meant that my job was getting even safer. Yes, so did I. However, many of us didn't count on the strange way high-level management sees the world. So after acquiring companies, then reorganising, many of us found ourselves without a job. After the six hard years that I had given to helping the company rebuild its computer systems, this was a kick in the guts.

With mortgage interest rates running at a record 17.5%, three young children in primary school and all of the other costs and responsibilities of having a young family, our seemingly good fortune had rapidly done an about face.

The next two years were a daily struggle to make ends meet and keep the bank happy. Donna, who had a wider range and more marketable set of skills than myself, was able to find a fulltime and part-time job. She spent her days working in a mail-sorting centre and her evenings behind a cash register at a service station. Meanwhile, I had found a job working in a factory making plastic parts for advertising units. On Saturdays, I was working on the gate at a trash 'n treasure market, hiring out display tables to stall holders and putting PAID stamps on the hands of customers. Exciting work it certainly wasn't, but at least between us it kept food in the mouths of the kids. I was to find out years later that during this period, Donna was going without food on occasions so the children and I could eat. She was well aware that, being diabetic, going without food was not an option for me. But I was unaware she was doing this at the time.

It seems almost archaic now, but 1993/4 was before the internet had become available to the general public. I know, hard to imagine, isn't it? We take so much for granted now, like instant access to available jobs, near instant contact through email, sending an application and resume online, but in 1993/4, this simply didn't exist. Because of this, finding a job was done the old-fashioned way, by buying the Saturday broadsheet newspaper and laboriously working through the job ads. This became a regular activity, but unlike sending off an email, it involved multiple steps.

1. Circle potential jobs in the newspaper.
2. Adjust the standard application cover letter according to the advertisement.
3. Make any tweaks required to the resume to highlight a certain skill or experience.
4. Print off the cover letter and resume.
5. Go to the post office and buy a presentation folder, large envelope and stamp.
6. Write the address for the prospective job on the envelope.
7. Place the bundle of documents into the envelope, ensuring everything was correct and neat.
8. Seal the envelope, stick the stamp on the front and then take it to the counter for posting.
9. Wait for at least a week before getting any response. Of course these rarely came. That part of the process hasn't changed.

Over a two-year period, I completed this process over 50 times, sometimes posting off five applications, sometimes only one. Another surprising aspect to this process, looking back over those 20 years, was how expensive it was to apply for a professional job when you were unemployed. There was the paper for the printer, the large envelope, the presentation folder and the stamp. Plus, there was the petrol required to get all of this done and the time required. Back then, the post office was only open from 9:30 a.m. until 4 p.m., Monday to Friday. This made it exceptionally difficult if you had found a fill-in job, as I had.

Donna and I persisted with this laborious process for two years. Australia was deeply involved in the 'Recession we had to have' as, to again quote our prime minister of the time, we were verging on becoming a 'banana republic'. There was a lot of pain required for Australia to work its way through the bad times and come out the other side. Unfortunately, my family and many others were caught in the mess and had to do what was necessary to survive.

Then one day… Ahhhh, what a day!

The telephone rang. No big deal; the telephone rang many times during the day. I picked it up and said hello, to be met by a silence with the tell-tale hiss of a long distance call. Don't forget that this was back in the pre-internet days when mobile phones were rare and long-distance calls almost as rare.

"Hello."

"Could I please speak with Mr Alex Williams?"

"Speaking."

(Clearing of throat on the phone) "Some time ago, you applied for a job in Saudi Arabia."

This was news to me. Having applied for over 50 jobs over the past two years, I couldn't be expected to remember each and every one.

(Clearing of throat by me) "Yes, that is correct."

"My name is Brian (forgotten) from Riyad Bank. I'm calling in relation to your application. Are you still interested in the job?"

Now let me see. I'm working in a factory during the week and stamping people's hands on the weekend. Donna is working two jobs and we rarely get to see each other. And the bank is not far from knocking on the door.

"Yes, I'm still interested."

"OK, good. I have a couple of questions."

He then proceeded to ask me a few questions regarding my knowledge around the technical requirements for the job. Keep in mind that I had now been out of the computer industry for over two years, so my technical skills were either rusty or, even worse, out-of-date. I was able to provide the stock standard generic answers to the first few questions, so, so far so good. Then he asked a question that nearly killed my prospects.

"What can you tell me about Endevor processors?"

I focused on the word 'processors', thinking instead of the word 'processes'. I thought this was an odd question but proceeded to explain in generic terms about the processes surrounding the technical activity. Then suddenly I had one of those flash moments.

Processes? Processors? Endevor? He's not asking about processes, you idiot! He's asking about Endevor processors!

"Hold on a moment," I said. "You're asking about Endevor processors," and then proceeded to provide a two-sentence description of what an Endevor processor was and what it did. I found out months later that it was that moment and that answer that had secured the job for me. My family's and my economic and emotional welfare had pivoted right at that moment in time. I had begun to stumble, which would have blown my chances with the job, but at the last moment, I had saved the situation and had given the correct answer.

"Thank you, Alex," said Brian. "Someone will be in contact soon."

After going through the standard pleasantries, we finished the call.

"How did it go?" asked Donna.

"I don't know, but I think it went well. We'll have to wait and see."

Three days later, the phone rang again. There was the delay and the hiss indicating a long-distance call. My heart leapt into my throat.

"Hello."

"Hello. Could I please speak with Mr Alex Williams?"

"Speaking."

"Hello. My name is Abdul (forgotten) and I work for Al-Khaleej Consultants." My breath got caught in my throat. I had no idea who I was talking to and had never heard of a company called Al-Khaleej Consultants. But I knew that I was talking to someone associated with The Middle East and so was frozen as I held the phone to my head.

"Al-Khaleej is acting on behalf of Riyad Bank and they would like to offer you the job of operations consultant."

I felt woozy and my head went light. Could I really be hearing what I was hearing? Was I really being offered a job in Saudi Arabia?

"That's good to hear," I said.

"We will be sending you a letter with some details and a ticket for the flight to Dammam. The plan is that you will be spending some time in Dammam, getting to know the system, and will then be transferring to Riyadh. Does all of that sound OK?" What was I going to say? I mean, really. I'd been effectively unemployed for going on to three years; I'd been working fill-in jobs to bring in some money and remain active; my wife had worked her fingers to the bone making ends meet. What was I going to say?

"Yes, that sounds good."

"OK, then we will be in touch," he said before ending the call.

"So…?" asked Donna, who had been listening quietly from another room.

"They've offered me the job," I said, still dumbfounded from the telephone conversation I had just finished.

"What is it?" asked Donna.

"I'm not really sure," I said honestly. "It's in a place called Riyadh, or Dammam, in Saudi Arabia and they want me there in the next few weeks."

"Are you going to go?" she asked.

"Well, yeah. I don't think we really have a choice."

The Magic Kingdom

It was a hectic four weeks before I found myself in Saudi Arabia.

With such a whirlwind of organising with passports, airline tickets, visas and a plethora of other details, my head stayed up in the clouds for days after my arrival. Coming from Brisbane, Australia, and landing in Dhahran, Saudi Arabia, culture shock doesn't really explain the avalanche of impressions and emotions. In 1995, the first impression that a new arrival from Australia to Saudi Arabia got as they disembarked from the plane at the airport in Dhahran was the heat. The flight arrived early in the morning, at about one o'clock, and after grabbing my cabin luggage, I walked down the stairs of the plane to the tarmac, along with the many other jetlagged passengers. There to greet us was a line of the huge, weird looking airport buses that can be found at many airports around the world.

Crammed on to the bus were dazed-looking people, predominantly men, from all over the world, each gripping their cabin luggage. I found myself surrounded by people from Indonesia, Bangladesh, India, the Philippines, plus one or two other Aussies and Kiwis. No one was in a chatting mood as we were all in the same dazed state of mind.

The bus was soon at the entrance to the check-in hall, where we all grabbed our bags again and shuffled off the bus and into the hall. This was where I encountered the next overwhelming impression that told me I was no longer in the closeted safety of Australia. As we shuffled forward to join the long queues of people waiting to check in, I had a real sense of being in a Saturday afternoon movie with Gregory Peck or Charlton Heston, as there were quite a few guys in the lines wearing strange head gear and loin cloths. We could see many khaki uniformed guards with machine guns over their shoulders. I remembered back to all of the people back in Oz who had either expressed their personal concern about my safety or just outright advised me not to go. The impression that we are fed by the media in Oz is that the Middle East, and particularly Saudi Arabia, are dangerous places where any clear-thinking Australian would not choose to go. And here I was standing in a hot, humid, cavernous shed in the middle of the night with hundreds of people from exotic parts of the world, some wearing exotic clothing, staring down a long line of new arrivals, all being watched over by serious-looking fellows with machine guns.

I stood there, looked around and a scene from The Wizard of Oz came to mind. "Toto, I've a feeling we're not in Kansas anymore."

Eventually, after a lot of checking, unpacking, packing and stamping of passports, I found myself out on the public side of the door. In 1995, the airport at Dhahran, which was the gateway to Saudi from anywhere in Asia, Australia and New Zealand, was not a great introduction to the country. It was old, rundown, a little bit smelly and just had a musty feel about it. After the long flight and the last 90 minutes of passport control and queuing, now stepping out to see a rather drab forecourt, my excitement level had not yet started to rise. Fortunately, I had no problem finding the driver holding a sign with my name on it, so was soon on my way to the hotel.

I don't know about you, but I am always fascinated when I arrive in a new city. For some reason, it's always at night, with the exception of London. But everywhere else I've flown to from Australia, it's always night when we arrive. And with the flight landing at one in the morning, the time taken going through the process at the airport, then finding my car and driver, it was 3:30 in the morning as we drove from the airport to the hotel that they had put me in for the rest of the night. Consequently, the city was quiet.

It seemed like forever that we were driving up near-empty freeways, then turning onto deserted surface roads. The street lights were glowing yellow and what I could see from their light was quite different to the impression I had got from peering down from the window of the plane. Up there, everything was neatly laid out, with the freeways sweeping in graceful curves around the city. But from down here, it was clear that I was now in a third world country. Saudi doesn't like to consider itself a third world country. It has huge oil reserves and has spent a large fortune on infrastructure over the past 50 years. But at street level at four o'clock in the morning driving down deserted roads, it was easy to see that it wasn't far removed from being just that.

At least now I could tell the naysayers back home that the streets are paved, not sand or gravel, and I didn't see any mud brick buildings on the drive from the airport and I didn't see a single camel. However, I was certainly going to be seeing lots of each of these before my time in Saudi Arabia was finished.

For a diabetic, one of the difficulties with travelling across time zones is the adjustment of medication times. Depending on the flight details, there is both the ongoing adjustment necessary while travelling and then the final adjustment after you arrive at your destination. The time difference between Brisbane and Saudi Arabia is eight hours, but the flight is broken in the middle with a stopover in Singapore. It's not easy to explain to a person who doesn't have to live with it, the importance, the danger, the concern that the diabetic has while making the adjustments. Having insulin is not like taking a pill for a headache. Having an injection of insulin is more like squirting high-octane fuel into the engine of a drag car. Insulin is not a fuel, but it's the best example I can think of right now.

If you don't squirt enough of the fuel into the engine, it will simply stop. But if you squirt too much fuel, the engine will momentarily run too fast before exploding. But, and here's the scary bit, when an insulin dependent diabetic is doing long-distance flights, timing their insulin injections is like trying to squirt in just enough fuel into the engine of the drag car while it's in the process of doing its ¼ mile run. Too little and their blood sugar level runs high; too much and they risk having a hypo, i.e., severe low blood sugar level and its immediate dangers. But now complicate that by changing time zones and day becomes night, breakfast becomes dinner and midnight becomes lunch time.

So after a couple of hours of fitful sleep, I had to very carefully time my morning routine. I knew that I was being picked up by the company driver at nine o'clock, so I knew that I had to not only ensure that I was presentable for my first day on the job at a new company, but I also had to make sure that I had my morning insulin no sooner than 15 to 20 minutes before I would have my breakfast available to me. I was also working on the assumption that the breakfast would have enough carbohydrate for me. Keep in mind that I had arrived at the hotel at four o'clock in the morning, so had not been able to check the things that most people just take for granted or dismiss as unimportant, such as availability of food. Having just arrived in the country, all I had with me were the remnants of my emergency travelling food. If necessary that would be enough to see me through until the driver arrived, and then I would ask him to stop at a food shop of some sort. But as this was my first day on the job, I didn't want to start by causing unexpected difficulties.

People often say, when they hear about this sort of situation, "Oh yes, but they need to know that you need your food and that you need…" Yes, that is correct, but when you live with type 1 diabetes every minute of every day of your life, the dynamics of these situations take on a different colour. I don't feel that I need to hide my diabetes, not at all. But conversely, I also don't want my diabetes to become what people think of when my name is mentioned or they are in my company. It's hard enough having to juggle the insulin, food and energy requirements every minute of every day, without adding the complications of making those around you think of you as 'the diabetic'.

With all of these unknown factors and concerns, my first morning in The Magic Kingdom went without a hitch. I did manage to make myself presentable, and I did manage to have my insulin injection, followed by an acceptable breakfast within the right timeframe. The little wrinkles that often present themselves didn't let me down this time either. There wasn't enough carbohydrate in the continental breakfast offered by the hotel, but I was able to obtain a glass of orange juice to boost it up. Exciting stuff, huh? But sadly, that sort of mundane detail becomes vital to a diabetic.

After a short stop over at the company office, where I was introduced to too many people whose names I didn't have a chance of remembering, the driver took myself and my luggage off to the accommodation that had been arranged for me. The plan was that I'd be spending a couple of months in Dammam, which is on the east coast of Saudi Arabia, then moving to the head office of the bank, which is in Riyadh. Riyadh is the capital city of Saudi Arabia and is 400 km into the desert. I was fascinated at the prospect of that new adventure, but for now I had the new city of Dammam to get to know.

It took 15 minutes of carnival ride to get to my temporary accommodation. I didn't know which way to look; there was just so much to see. By first impressions, Dammam is not a pretty city, but it was new to me, it was exotic and it was exciting. Having never been overseas before, except to New Zealand, this was my first out-of-Australia experience. I thought Singapore on the way over was exciting, but this took it to a whole new level. Everywhere I looked, I could see guys dressed in the flowing white robes with the red and white checkered headgear. I was soon to learn that most of those fellows are Saudis, as all Saudi men wear the *'thobe'* (white robe) and *'shumagg'* (read and white head covering). I could also see the occasional woman wearing the flowing black robes, which I came to learn is called an *'abaya'*.

After we arrived, the driver knocked on the door of the unit I was to be sharing with another Australian. I stood back and waited a moment before the door was opened. The driver started introducing himself and explaining who I was, but I just stood there with my mouth hanging open. Because who should have opened the door but my best friend from high school, George. I kid you not. There we were on the other side of the planet and George opened the door.

Well, you can imagine how the next few hours were spent. "Do you remember when…? And I wonder what happened to…." We had a lot of catching up to do. Fortunately for me, George was able to introduce me to many of the things to do with Saudi Arabia that a newbie from Oz finds confusing or confronting. He was also able to explain the intricate workings of the work situation, the relationship between the company we were both working for and the bank that we were working at. I felt a bit silly, to be honest, that I wasn't already clear on much of this, but I was to learn over the next five years that most westerners arrive in Saudi for the first time in a similar dazed and naïve state of mind.

One of the curious things that George was able to explain to me that very first evening was when we went to a local shopping mall. As we were walking around, seeing Saudi families out doing the same thing, I noticed that there were many young Saudi fellows walking through the mall holding hands. Coming from Australia, I drew an immediate conclusion from that.

I nudged George in the ribs and whispered, "I thought that sort of thing was against the law in Saudi." He laughed and said that it is. However, what I was seeing was a local custom where male friends hold hands in some social settings, like walking through a shopping mall. Coming from Australia, where that would only have one conclusion, I found this quite interesting. Before my time in Saudi Arabia was finished five years later, I was to learn hundreds or thousands of interesting tidbits of information about Saudi, the Arabian Peninsula, the Arabic people, their culture and their language. I also learnt a lot about western cultures and people. But that might be for another story one day.

The original plan was that I would stay with George in Dammam for three months, but it soon became apparent that it wasn't necessary. By the way, the names Dammam, Al-Khobar and Dhahran are almost interchangeable, as together they form a large urban area on the east coast of Saudi Arabia across from Bahrain. The plan was that I would use this time to become more acquainted with the computer operations side of the business. I soon realised that my main focus was going to be with the IT workers in Riyadh, not Dammam, so started the cogs turning so I could move there. After only four weeks in Dammam, I found myself on a plane to Riyadh.

I was to find that many westerners in Saudi vigorously prefer Dammam to Riyadh. Their reasoning is that because Dammam is Shiite and Riyadh Sunni, Dammam is easier going and accepting of western customs. For example, it is quite common in Dammam for western women to go shopping in one of the shopping malls without covering up with the *abaya*. However, in Riyadh, that is a definite no, no. Many westerners, both male and female, find that alone is enough for them to not like Riyadh and prefer Dammam. Donna and I never saw that sort of thing as a problem. We went to Saudi Arabia expecting things to be different and were not greatly surprised when they were.

For me, Riyadh was the place to be. I loved it. Mind you, it was difficult for me to settle in, with me even contemplating leaving and flying home during the first couple of months there. But after teething problems with the accommodation and finding a group of expats that I got along well with, I was eventually able to bring some stability into my week-to-week life.

Why I preferred Riyadh to Dammam was because of a number of things. Firstly, it was 400 km into the desert. Riyadh in 1995 was a city of over a million people, with all of the things that a large population requires. And yet it was 400 km into the desert from the east coast. I find that fascinating. Also, Riyadh is the seat of government for Saudi Arabia. It is the centre of power for this fascinating country and is the main residence for the king of Saudi Arabia. Plus it is BECAUSE Riyadh follows the more conservative side of Islam that Donna and I preferred to be there; of course Donna after she and the girls joined me there in 1996. We didn't travel halfway around the planet to pretend we were still in suburban Brisbane. We learnt how other people and cultures live, how their view of the world is both similar to ours and differs from ours. We learnt that, even though we were living in a city that has the infamous 'Chop Chop Square', where convicted criminals are occasionally beheaded, the local people are friendly people devoted to their families and in so many ways no different to us. I could wax lyrical on this subject for hours, but that is not the purpose of this story, so I shall leave it there. In summary, my family and I fell in love with Riyadh and the Arabic culture.

One thing that Riyadh also had was a shortage of easily accessible forms of entertainment for your typical western families. This was another aspect of Saudi Arabia that many westerners had a problem with. In both Dammam and Riyadh, and I'm guessing Jeddah as well, there were no cinemas. Nope, none. Zero. Yes, you heard correctly. Plus there were no places like clubs or discos that you could go for a drink and a dance. And of course that raises possibly the biggest issue that some westerners have about Saudi Arabia and that is that the whole country is dry, i.e., no alcohol was legally permitted within the country. There was no grey area on this subject at all. Alcohol is banned within the borders of Saudi Arabia.

But this is where Donna and I and the girls might be a little different to some other people, in that none of this bothered us too much. We soon learnt to make do with what was available and to make our own fun. There were videos to replace cinemas and heaps of restaurants to go to. There were fascinating and exotic markets, called souks, to go to as well. As for alcohol, well… I won't go into detail, but let's just say that virtually every westerner soon learnt how to overcome that strict rule. It was actually quite humorous the various ways that people managed to provide the expat community with a range of liquid joy. And this was another aspect of living in Riyadh that was so good, and that was living the expat life. Throw a bunch of westerners together and they soon learn to establish a sense of community more colourful and vibrant than life back home. This was one of the aspects of our time in Riyadh that Donna particularly loved.

A significant part of 'making our own fun', that had been vital for helping me get through the first 12 months without Donna and the girls, was going out of Riyadh for trips to the desert. As I've already described, Riyadh is 400 km into the desert, so it is completely surrounded by desert of some sort. And with five or six major highways into and out of Riyadh from other cities in Saudi Arabia, there were heaps of opportunities to go exploring.

This is where the majority of western expats drew the line. I estimate that 90% of western expats went to the desert at least once in their time in Riyadh. But only 60% went twice. When you consider those who went on, let's say a monthly basis, you'd be down to 10% or less. During the first couple of months that I was in Riyadh before the family came over, a large part of the difficulties I was facing came from a combination of the limited range of activities available that did NOT require large amounts of liquid joy, the unwillingness of most of the guys I was living with in the block of units to commit themselves to a weekend activity and then follow through, combined with the afore mentioned reluctance of most expats to go to the desert. Since a child, I've always been into walking and exploring, so to keep myself sane, I had to work out some way of getting out to the desert. I had a car; that wasn't a problem. The problem was finding someone to go with.

Over the next couple of months, my state of mind deteriorated to the point where Donna was suggesting I give up and come home during our weekly telephone calls. I wasn't about to do that, but that's how bad I sounded to her on the phone. My state of mind wasn't dangerous; I was just lonely and frustrated. I could see a solution but couldn't find anyone to enable me to put it into action.

The crisis point was reached one Thursday morning, which in Saudi Arabia is equivalent to our Saturday morning.

I had arranged with a couple of the other fellows who lived in the block of units that we were going for a drive to the desert. I had ensured that they were committed and clear on departure time, etc. I even made the clear understanding that they needed to bring a bit of food and water, as we were leaving the city and they wouldn't have an opportunity to buy any. Everyone agreed and life was looking good.

On Wednesday night, which is the equivalent to our Friday night, work was finished for the week, so there was the usual barbeque and party at the block of units. A goodly group of expat single males was there to party the night away. I noticed that a couple of the guys who were coming to the desert the next day were well into the party, so I reminded them of the activity the next day and they confirmed that it was still on and they'd be there.

Let's leave out the rest of the night's partying because we all know what a night like that usually becomes. Instead we'll jump forward to 9 o'clock the next morning, with me sitting out in the common area waiting for them, ready to go. Ooze forward now to 10 o'clock, with no change in the scenario. Take another step to 11 o'clock.

That's it! I'd had it! I couldn't take any more. I stormed off with a dramatic banging of doors and went for a drive to calm myself down and consider what I was going to do about this appalling situation. This was now do-or-die. This situation had the potential to kill the whole Saudi episode for my family and I and that would be a disaster.

I drove around the city for a while and finally found myself in the DQ, or Diplomatic Quarter. This is the part of the city where most of the foreign embassies exist. Foreigners were allowed to go there at any time, while locals were either not allowed to go, or needed to justify to the guards on the entrance gate why they wished to enter.

The DQ was enormous, the size of a whole suburb. It had its own shops, parks and gardens as well as the many embassies and other official buildings. It was in the DQ where you would find the embassy for the U.S.A., for Britain, for Australia, New Zealand, etc. Not surprisingly, it was not difficult to identify the embassy of the U.S.A. Even in 1995, it was all of the following—the biggest, the most elaborate, had the most impressive gardens, appeared to have the most guards and also had the most in-your-face concrete barricades and uniformed guards with big guns in plain view. Of course it also had a big American flag on a big flagpole. Conversely, the Australian embassy while certainly nice, was smaller, unobtrusive, not easy to find unless you knew where to look and overall subtle. Ya gotta love the Americans.

I found a peaceful-looking place to park the car and sit out on the grass. Yes, the DQ also had possibly the only proper grass lawns in all of Riyadh. So I chose a peaceful, quiet place to sit and think and contemplate the next few months.

At this point in my Saudi experience, it had not been determined whether Donna and the girls could come over. All of that discussion was yet to eventuate. All I knew at that point was that I was there on my own. I was very lonely and I was going not-so-slowly nuts. If I was to stay and survive, I needed to have something to plan for and look forward to.

Over the weeks I'd been there, I had never heard anyone say that they had been to the desert on their own. What I had heard was lots of inference that precisely the opposite was true, i.e., the desert was not somewhere that one should venture by themselves. But then the attitude of most of the westerners was that you simply don't leave the city, simple as that, so in my mind that threw into question many of the general attitudes of the westerners. I had now been forced to the point where I needed to think outside the square. Standard solutions had not worked. So by process of logic, clarity and elimination, I came to the conclusion that I had to learn how to go to the desert on my own. Suddenly I felt much happier. I had a mission, a challenge, an objective, a goal. On the face of it, that may not sound like a big decision. So what, go to the desert on my own? Big deal. But when you consider that temperatures in Saudi Arabia easily reach 50C, the desert stretched for hundreds of kilometres in every direction around Riyadh, there was almost nothing in the desert except many things that could kill a car and that there were very few people to be seen in these hundreds of kilometres of nothing, it was a big decision; many would say stupid.

Over the next week, I asked lots of questions of anyone who would stand still long enough. The most important thing that I learnt, something that could derail the whole endeavour, was that the government had an expectation that westerners did not need to travel outside the city of their work. Now this is where people who haven't experienced Saudi Arabia can easily develop a bad opinion of the place, but the reality is not as bad as the explanation sounds.

Every person in Saudi Arabia has what is known as an *iqama*. This is nothing more than what a lot of countries have, which is an official form of identification. All Muslims have a green *iqama* and all non-Muslims have a brown *iqama*.

On each of the highways in and out of each city, there are checkpoints. Yes, I know; this is starting to sound like communist Russia or Nazi Germany, but the reality is much more benign and unexciting. As you stop at the checkpoint, you needed to show your *iqama* to the guard. He may also ask for your driver's licence and car registration papers, which were always kept in the glove box. If you are not a Saudi citizen, he may also have asked for your travel papers, which was simply an official letter from your employer stating, in Arabic, that you were entitled to travel outside the city. Similar to the 'don't ask/don't tell' official attitude to the liquid joy, the official attitude to the travel letter was that, so long as it was written properly, on official letter head, stating that the holder had an employment related reason for travelling outside the city, no further questions would be asked. It was as simple as that. In my five years of driving the length and breadth of Saudi Arabia, I was never asked to show my travel letter.

So that became my main requirement for that week. Off I went to see Mohammed, a charming fellow from Pakistan whose reason for existing was to organise 'stuff' like paperwork, official letters, airline tickets, travel documents and general semi-official advice for the westerners. I asked him what I needed to do to get a letter saying I could travel outside Riyadh. He had been asked for this hundreds of times over the years, so he understood that it was important for many westerners to not feel restricted too much or cooped up. The bank needed the westerners, and Mohammed took it upon himself to keep the westerners happy. It was a very sad day for us when he told us that he had finally received his green card and he and his family were leaving Saudi and moving to the U.S.A.

So, by the end of that week, I had my official travel letter, which was maybe the single most important piece of paper I would have during the whole five years in The Magic Kingdom, with the exception of my final airline ticket home.

Next came the logistical planning for my first foray into this unknown and scary place called 'the desert'. I decided on it being the coming weekend for my first trip and had a lot of thinking and organising to do, not least being deciding where to go. Talking to my fellow westerners, I heard the name 'Hidden Valley' mentioned on numerous occasions. I also heard names such 'The Edge of the World' and 'The Empty Quarter' mentioned. But the two most often mentioned pieces of advice were Hidden Valley and a book of desert trips around Riyadh that was available that had been written and published some years earlier by an enterprising westerner.

Interestingly, there was little point asking any of my Saudi work mates for guidance, even though they would have been more than happy to give me advice. You see, where I was planning to go and what I was planning to do wasn't anything special for them. Some of them had grown up living in the type of desert I was planning to go to. And I was to learn that what we called desert, they referred to as farm land. I kid you not! One time when I described a particularly spectacular place that I had visited over a weekend to one of my Saudi work mates, he gave me an incredulous look and told me that his family farms camels and goats there, so it wasn't a desert. Believe me when I say that to anyone visiting Saudi Arabia from outside the Arabic Peninsular, what I had seen that weekend was a vast, spectacular, awe-inspiring desert.

By the Wednesday evening, the where, what and how for my first solo foray into the Saudi Arabian desert had been organised. This included a backpack, bottles of water, lots of food, a hat and other obvious safety gear, plus the book of desert trips. I was to determine years later that I was hopelessly unprepared on that first journey, but luckily for me, that didn't matter.

So much about Riyadh was fascinating back then. Apart from being the centre of one of the more unknown and closed off countries in the world, the evidence of almost limitless money was everywhere. Over the following years, I learnt a lot more about the recent and brief history of modern Saudi Arabia, but that first drive out of the city was a real journey into the unknown for me.

After navigating my way to the outskirts of the city, I found myself on a six lane freeway hurtling along at 120 kph. That was the sign-posted speed, but many drivers seemed to simply ignore that and go blasting past me. As I was driving the rental car, which was a Hyundai Excel with a small four cylinder engine, I soon learnt to stay out of the fast lane. That was where the bigger cars were powering past way in excess of 120 kph. I didn't stand a chance there. Over time I also learnt to stay out of the slow lane, as this is where the many trucks trundle up and down the freeway. In summer, when the air temperature often reaches 50C, the bitumen can start to melt. And with the heavy trucks travelling in the slow lane, the surface of the road took on what, in a small car, was a frightening carnival ride appearance. The trucks left serious grooves in the bitumen during summer, making the slow lane a dangerous place to be in any standard type of car. Even 4WD cars, with their bigger wheels and more robust suspension, could struggle in the slow lane.

So the middle lane it was as I left Riyadh behind. I didn't get a clear idea of my surroundings on that first drive out of the city, as it was all too new to me and there were simply too many things to look at. But I was to learn as time went on that Riyadh is surrounded by new areas that are being turned into suburbs. It was fast becoming a large and significant city. One of the differences that having almost limitless money gave Saudi Arabia, compared to what we are used to in Australia, is that when they decide to allocate a section of land for a new housing development, they build all of the infrastructure first, then open it to the housing developers. So I was driving past vast areas where all of the roads, footpaths, power supply, water supply, sewerage and telephone had already been built. All that was left to do now was to build the houses and shops. But I'm not talking about an acre or two. I'm talking about entire suburbs that stretched away from the freeway for kilometres, where everything was in place except for the buildings. And it was all just sitting there like it had been for years.

I learnt that the Saudi government managed its oil wealth for the benefit of the country by having five year plans. Each five-year plan would have main focus points, like building hospitals or building universities and schools. Obviously a previous five-year plan had a focus for establishing suburbs, so all of the infrastructure was there and now it just waited for private industry to catch up and build the houses. The six lane freeway that I was on that carved its way through the desert in great, sweeping curves was part of an earlier five-year plan. I came to learn that the whole country was criss-crossed by a network of modern freeways and highways, connecting all of the major cities and towns.

Eventually, I left the waiting-to-be-built-on suburbs behind as I continued heading west. But I hadn't gone far before the road descended at a steep grade. Over in the slow lane, the many trucks were now crawling down the hill in low gear and the smell of burning brakes and clutch plates was quite apparent. For the rest of us in the middle lane, we just continued to descend at 120 kph, while those big boys in the fast lane went rocketing past at whatever speed they wanted to drive.

This is where we'll look at another aspect of Saudi Arabia that most westerners point at and cluck their disappointment. All of the drivers of every vehicle on the road was male. Not a single female driver was to be seen anywhere. The reason for that is that, at that time, women were not allowed to drive in Saudi Arabia. Yes, it's true. None of that urban legend or hearsay is incorrect. Now I'm not going to justify the Saudi government's law but just say that, in 1995, that was the case. Pressure is afoot now in 2014 to change that situation, but to date, it has not yet succeeded in changing the law in Saudi Arabia.

Also, speaking of big boys in the fast lane, one of the curious things that I saw many times over the years while driving the length and breadth of Saudi Arabia was that the super-rich, such as princes, government ministers, their sons and other rich businessmen, seemed to have the freedom to drive their super-rich cars, like top-end Mercedes, Ferraris, Rolls Royces, Porches, you name it, as fast as they liked in the fast lane. It was common to see someone coming up from behind in the fast lane, flashing their lights furiously at whoever happened to be ahead of them. As they blew past slow old me doing 120 kph in the middle lane, they had to have been doing in excess of 200 kph, still flashing their lights and without slowing down a jot. It was comical to watch, unless you were the poor sod who had dared to pull into the fast lane to go past a slow coach in the middle doing only 110. You can take my word for it that a Hyundai Excel doesn't accelerate rapidly from 110 to 120, no matter how hard you push the accelerator to the floor. I quickly learnt to stay out of the fast lane unless absolutely necessary. This was particularly the case when driving on the 400 km, six-lane freeway from Riyadh to Dammam.

The big descent that I was now going down was known as German Cutting. The reason for this was something to do with the company that designed the freeway and the cutting being a German company, so the westerners simply knew it as German Cutting. It became an important landmark when planning days out in the desert. The conversation would go something like: "You get to the bottom of German Cutting, then turn right. Travel for another five kilometres and you'll see a track beside a fence." For this first trip, when I was hoping to find Hidden Valley, I needed to get to the bottom of German Cutting, then turn left.

About halfway down German Cutting, which enables the freeway to descend from the plateau on which Riyadh is situated to the vast expanse of the Arabian shield beyond, the road emerges from the cliff face in a long, steep swoop. As it does, you suddenly get a view of the area at the bottom of the cliff. In a flash of scenery change, I could suddenly see my first village, with its assortment of houses, mud-brick buildings, dirt roads, donkeys, a few camels dotted around, date palms and children riding their bikes. I could suddenly see all of this from above, so high was the escarpment and the road that I was on. This was my first view of Arabia outside of a big city, so I was now entering the real Arabia and my heart jumped. It was only now that I fully realised that I was starting a true adventure, one that would last for another five years.

The Desert—A Love Story

After turning left off the freeway—oh, let me take a break here and describe something else that I find quirky. Our network of freeways in Australia is not a smudge on what I'm told they are in the USA. Yes, we have freeways, but until recently they've mainly been for connecting point A to point B. It was only ten or fifteen years ago that they started to connect up into the beginnings of a network. In Saudi Arabia, they had all this oil money and they needed to rapidly modernise their country, so they brought in experts from all over the world to help them build a modern infrastructure, hence German Cutting.

But America being the home of the freeway, the Saudis had obviously brought in experts from the USA to help them design their freeways, which resulted in some very impressive engineering feats. Riyadh has a spectacular junction of freeways and highways, which the westerners call 'Spaghetti Junction'. It's one of those landmarks that westerners use to navigate around the city.

But even a simple intersection of a freeway and a highway out of the city was designed by the experts with the future in mind, so it had a full clover-leaf intersection. In 1995, it wouldn't surprise me to learn that Australia was yet to build its first clover-leaf intersection. So I hadn't experienced the need to do a 270-degree loop in order to join the cross road. Plus keep in mind that in Australia we drive on the left hand side of the road, but in Saudi Arabia they drive on the right hand side, so their roads are designed accordingly. It took me a long time to get used to turning left from a freeway to a cross road on a clover-leaf intersection, by doing a right hand exit followed by a full 270 degree right hand turn. It never became natural to me in my whole stay in Saudi Arabia.

OK, so I had just turned left from the freeway and was now driving along the minor road, looking for the next turn to the right. I had no idea where I was going, except that the map in the book was telling me what to watch out for. Now that I was at the bottom of the escarpment, I was surrounded by impressive rock formations, all weathered and gnarled by the centuries of wind and sand. I didn't know whether to look left or right, so I drove slowly and tried to look at everything.

Eventually, I had travelled the distance dictated by the book, and could now see a gravel track going off to the left. At this point, it looked like a simple gravel road, so I didn't hesitate to turn my little rental car onto it and continue away from the main road. Ahead of me the gravel road climbed gently until it went over the top of a rise about a kilometre away, so I carefully drove towards that point. By now, I was 50 kilometres from Riyadh driving a Hyundai Excel with a 1.2 litre motor and standard tyres, driving along a gravel road heading further into the desert. What I didn't need at this point was a flat tyre, an overheating engine or a rock through the sump.

It wasn't long before I got to the top of the rise and found that the gravel road deteriorated gradually to a gravel track that continued on around a few winds and turns. There were now rocks and holes in the track that I needed to carefully steer around. What I also found was that the track was descending into a small valley of some sort, with almost vertical cliffs on either side. At the bottom of the cliffs, which were roughly 30 metres high, were many large boulders that had broken away from them over the eons. As I carefully drove further, I could see the cliffs gradually widening out. I knew now that I was in Hidden Valley and could easily see how it got its name.

The landscape in that small valley, for a first time visitor who was a keen bush walker at home, was mesmerising. I slowly drove along the track trying to look in every direction at once. Going off the main valley on both sides were other small valleys. Every twist and turn in the track found another treasure to investigate. A number of times I was so busy trying to absorb everything that I was seeing that I almost drove off the track or hit a rock. Luckily, I was crawling along as slow as I could go, so I wouldn't have done much damage anyway, but inadvertently damaging the car at this point in the proceedings was not a good idea.

After crawling along for 15 minutes, I finally decided that it was time to stop the car and go exploring on foot. I pulled off the track and opened the door, only to be smacked in the face by a wall of heat. I had been driving with the car window down, but I had also been sitting in the shaded protection of the car. Once out of the car and on foot, I was exposed to the full force of the sun. And even though this was only early summer, it still had a force that I wasn't expecting. One redeeming feature of the summer heat of the desert around Riyadh is that, being 400 km inland, the humidity is zero. We found it amazing when we went to Dammam just how much hotter it felt. Zero humidity compared to 100% humidity is a vast difference.

I gathered my stuff together in my backpack and took off to the right on foot. The floor of the valley, or *'whadi'* in Arabic, was covered in rocks, so walking was difficult. And the rocks were sharp and brutal. There was very little plant life, but there were scrubby looking bushes with huge needles on them for self-protection. There were also one or two strange looking small trees with papery bark that simply peeled off. These strange trees had large, leathery green leaves and I was to learn later that the westerners call them Scrotum trees. Later in the year, the trees were to bare large seed pods, each with two large seeds inside, that had an uncanny resemblance to well, based on the name you can probably work it out for yourself.

I was in exploring heaven. I walked for what seemed like hours, over rocks, past cliffs, along narrow goat tracks, all the while slowly moving away from the car. At last, I sat down in whatever shade I could find to have a drink of water and turned my attention in the direction of the car.

It had vanished.

I thought I hadn't walked far, having walked very slowly and sat down and rested a number of times. But now, as I looked back towards the car, it simply wasn't there anymore.

This was my introduction to something that I saw others struggle with as well over the years, when I took newbies out for their first experience of the desert. As there are very few landmarks, or at least not the sort of landmarks that we are used to seeing in our home countries of Australia, New Zealand, the USA, Canada and particularly England and

Europe, our way of navigating is compromised. Even though we hardly ever consider it at home, we must subconsciously keep track of trees, light poles, fence corners, creeks etc., to have a subtle understanding of where we are and how far we have travelled. But in the desert, where most of those landmarks just don't exist, our in-built navigation system doesn't work. Here I was looking back in the direction of the car, expecting to see it half hidden behind a large, fallen boulder, and it had simply vanished.

I didn't panic, but I also can't say I wasn't concerned. Don't forget that this was my very first experience of exploring the desert, and now I couldn't see the car. To make things worse, as I looked back in the general direction of the car, I could see that there were two *whadis* coming together, but with their coming together bit pointing towards me. So I was now looking down two *whadis*. Which one had I walked along to get to where I was now standing? My gut told me it was the one on the right, but I couldn't be sure. I looked for anything that might be a landmark, such as a bush or peculiarly shaped rock, but there was nothing. It all looked the same! I was rapidly losing confidence that it was the *whadi* on the right that I had walked along.

I sat down again to collect my thoughts and calm down a bit. I wasn't in full panic, but I could see it coming over the horizon. I looked at the two *whadis* and, after some careful consideration, could see that the one on the left was coming slightly downhill to where I was, whereas the one on the right was generally levelled. I thought back over the last half hour to try to remember if I had walked down a hill at any point. I thought back over all of the giant rocks and boulders that I had climbed around and over and wondered how I could ever tell if I was going up or down. But I finally concluded that it wasn't likely that I had been coming downhill, so I decided to try the *whadi* on the right.

An hour later, I was back at the car and breathing a small sigh of relief. My choice of the right-hand *whadi* had been correct, and consequently I had found the car. It was a lot further than I had expected, causing me a number of times to reconsider my choice of the right-hand *whadi*, but I persevered and had finally found the car and safety again. This was a lesson for me that I was to call on again and again over the next five years in Saudi Arabia.

There was a funny episode some years later when my friend Nick and I took a Canadian newbie out for his first desert exploration walk. We were again in Hidden Valley, but this time many kilometres further along. We measured it once in the car and the Hidden Valley area is 92 km long. After having breakfast as the sun came up, which is a surreal experience in the desert, the three of us had set off for a long walk. We intended to be away from the car for six to eight hours, so had plenty of water and food.

After hours of walking and exploring, our Canadian friend was obviously getting weary, so we started heading back to the car. During the day, we had climbed cliffs, crossed over the high point from one cliff to another, traversed a number of *whadis* and generally had a good time. We had stopped for lunch and boiled water for a cup of tea on a makeshift campfire. Nick and I had given Bill a grand introduction to the desert and the beauty of the country outside of Riyadh. But now it was time to be bringing the day's activities to a close.

As we emerged from a *whadi* and faced the huge expanse of the greater Hidden Valley, Bill looked along the valley and could see a bright sparkle. He gasped with relief and gushed that it was the sun reflecting off the windscreen, so we were almost there now. He then proceeded to hurry along towards the car so he could enjoy the comfort of a soft seat and some shade. I told him that we were further from the car than he might think and we still had a way to go, so he still needed to pace himself. He couldn't believe me and pointed at the car. "It's just there!" he said and scampered off in that direction. Nick and I looked at each other and shrugged our shoulders.

An hour and a half later, we reached the car. Bill was red in the face and way past his comfort zone. He flopped into the seat of the car and guzzled from the can of soft drink he had left behind for that purpose. He struggled to understand how the glint from the windscreen that he had seen was over 5 km away. That is one of the many astounding things about the desert. Nick and I loved it—Bill not so much that day.

Marathon des Sables—Long and Winding Road – 2008

"OK, so what's got you all excited?" asked Donna when I got home.

"Well," I said, as I hesitantly began the sales pitch, "I was reading in the paper on the way home that there's a big walk that I was thinking that I might do."

"Hmm?" she said, cautiously inviting further information.

"The thing is," I continued, "it's quite a big deal, and it won't be cheap."

"Yes?" she prompted.

"It's a 240 km endurance race over in the Sahara in Morocco." Donna looked at me with eyes that were slightly narrowed.

"When you say won't be cheap, how not cheap are we talking about?"

"Well," I said, "I was thinking that we could turn it into a holiday for us. You know, make it an opportunity to see a place we haven't been to yet. And Marrakesh has always been one of those exotic places that…." Donna held her hand up.

"You're starting to babble. If you're going to do this, you're going to do it properly. I would have some strict rules and would expect you to stick with them."

"Yes, of course," I blurted.

Donna continued, "Firstly, you're going to train properly. Secondly, you're going to go see the diabetes doctor and find out what you need to do to be prepared. Thirdly, you're going to go see a sports nutrition expert so you can work out the food. And last, you're not going to cut any corners. If you're going to do this, you're going to do it properly."

"Yes, OK," I said. What else could I say?

And with that, the Marathon des Sables adventure was underway.

Marathon des Sables— Preparation – 2008

I'd always been a bit of a walker. I enjoyed bushwalking and 'went bush' on the rare occasions when time and circumstances would allow. I had even had a stint at distance running when we were living in Brisbane. That only lasted for a year or so, until my knees and hips started to give me problems. From that experience, I learnt that the diabetes makes distance running difficult. Obviously with the number of marathon runners who have type 1 diabetes, distance running is not impossible, but it does have an extra dimension of difficulty and risk that, when combined with the deterioration of my knees and hips, meant that walking the Marathon des Sables and not running was a no-brainer. However, that wasn't going to be a problem because the event had been designed to allow for those who wished to walk. So long as you could maintain an average pace of 3.5 kph, you could complete each section within the allowed time.

The training started that same weekend. Now that I had the bug in my ear, I couldn't wait to get into it and was itching to get out there to start preparing. I had given myself two years to train, even though I thought that 12 months would have been ample, but I soon came to realise that I was going to need the whole two years. There was just so much to do.

The main lesson I learnt from my first few walks, which were only short stints of 5 km, was that I had a heck of a lot of work to do. I was old and wise enough by then to have realised that, even though I had been bushwalking for years, that didn't mean that I knew everything there was to know about endurance walking. Some years previously, in what could be looked at as a false start for the Marathon des Sables adventure, I had participated in the Oxfam Trailwalker 100 km walk for charity. I had trained hard for that and had thought that I was fully ready. Heck, at the start I even felt a bit sorry for the two young ladies who were part of our team of four, because they didn't have the bushwalking experience that I did and I thought they might not even finish. Well, did I end up eating my words?! They had been waiting at the finish line for myself and the other fellow for around an hour as he helped me stagger over the line in a state of almost complete collapse. To parody the words of Jack Nicholson to Tom Cruise in the movie *'A Few Good Men'*, *'Do you have a memory of that?'*, with Tom Cruise answering, *'Crystal!'* The memory of the finish line of the Oxfam Trailwalker was my base line for the Marathon des Sables. I must not put myself in that situation again.

From those early training walks, I reluctantly realised that the gear I was using was not good enough. My initial intention had been to not change a thing and dress in similar clothing, use the same boots and have the same backpack as I had always used for my bushwalks. I had many fond memories of delightful walks with this gear, both in Saudi Arabia and in Australia, so I considered it had been tested and proven.

Looking back now, that was an absurd thought, as were many of my initial thoughts as I was to learn. My boots were simply wrong, being too heavy and nowhere near tough enough. My backpack was all wrong, so needed to be upgraded. My clothes were wrong as they were too heavy and just not fit for purpose. And the food I was eating as I walked, to keep my sugar at an acceptable level, was also wrong. So after four weeks of training, I had learnt:

- My boots needed replacing.
- I needed a whole set of new clothes.
- My backpack needed replacing.
- I needed to learn about my food requirements for the desert.
- I needed to learn about my insulin requirements during endurance walking.
- I needed to toughen my feet and/or learn how to deal with blisters.

In essence, I was back to square one.

Entry to the Marathon Des Sables is not as easy as you may think. After hunting around on the internet, I was able to learn that, as the event is a French event, its primary focus is on having French people participating. Next in the order of preference were countries close to France, such as Spain, Germany, Netherlands, etc., so people from those countries received next preference for participation. This was followed by Great Britain and then the rest of the world. Over the years, the organisers had learnt that the best way to manage who could be part of this incredible event was to allocate spots to regions of the world. There was Western Europe, North

America, South America, and The Middle East, etc. Each region is allocated a number of places in the event and an agent is given the job of managing the booking process for each region. In 2008, Australia was part of the North American region, I suppose for reasons of language and simplicity, so I needed to work with a fellow in Colorado to get myself a place.

Unsurprisingly, my diabetes quickly became a potential sticking point. The agent in Colorado strongly recommended that, before progressing too far with the process, I get confirmation from the central management of the event in Paris that I would be allowed to participate. That was certainly easier said than done. First of all, I had to find a contact for the central management group, then had to overcome the language barrier. I came to find that, in a similar way to my French being effectively zero, not many French people speak English.

After many emails and a few late night phone calls to Paris, I was finally able to contact someone in the management team who spoke English. Then I had to explain to them why I was contacting them and that it was important that they understood the reason. All of this took a number of emails and phone calls, all the while with me fretting that I would miss out on making it onto the waiting list with the Colorado agent. He had explained that he ran the list on a first come/first serve basis, but even though I was one of the early ones to contact him about the 2010 event, there were already names on the list. So I was also racing against time to obtain confirmation from Paris.

Eventually, I either got lucky, or my persistence wore them down, but I was able to get a team doctor on the phone in Paris who was able to confirm that, so long as I fulfilled their extra requirements for fitness tests, related to my diabetes AND my age, they would not stop me from being part of the 2010 event. They would email me details of the extra fitness test requirements. It had taken a long time and a lot of frustration, but I had finally made it over that hurdle. I immediately passed that news back to the agent in Colorado so my name could be added to the list. It was then that I found that the marathon aspect of this event had already started, because before he could put my name of the waiting list, I had to get a 25% deposit to him.

I almost cried in frustration.

Once I calmed down, I thought about this latest road bump and decided that it was a reasonable request. The agent was running a business which spanned the USA, Canada, Australia, New Zealand and one or two other countries, so it was quite reasonable for him to want a financial commitment from people before putting their name on the list. But getting the money to him became the next issue.

As you can see, the marathon had already begun, without me even leaving my chair. Roadblocks like this littered the pathway in those first few months as I went through the paperwork and over hurdles just to get on the list. I was to find out later, after the dust and drama had settled from these early days, the agent had quietly been holding a spot open for me. I think he was as intrigued as the team doctors in Paris to see how I would go in the Sahara.

Doctor, I'm Walking Across the Sahara

One of Donna's requirements for giving me her permission to pursue this adventure was for me to have a full review of my diabetes management with a proper diabetes doctor, known as an endocrinologist. As I hadn't seen one for, ummm, way too long, that was a reasonable request.

"Hello Alex. How can we help you today?"

"Hi. I'm planning to walk across the Sahara desert and I'm here to find out what I need to do so I can complete this adventure without dying."

"You are planning to do what?"

"Walk across the Sahara."

"You have type 1 diabetes. You do know that you shouldn't be doing something like that, don't you?"

"Yes, I do. That's why I'm here, so I can learn what I need to."

This was how the 'Endo' and I started our discussion. She knew simply from the fact that I had been living with type 1 diabetes for 34 years, and was planning on walking across the Sahara, that I must have been doing something right for all those years. Many of the diabetics she saw daily, who had less years living with this illness under their belt, were in a much worse state of health than I was. Many would have been suffering with failing eyesight, failing kidneys, problems with their feet resulting in amputations along with other complications. And yet here was I proposing this wild adventure. So she let the normal doctor/patient routine drop and we began discussing the logistics of what I needed to do on a more even, one-to-one basis.

We talked about my history with type 1 diabetes so she could get a feel for how I manage it. She was also judging how much I knew about the biology of the illness and its management. I asked some questions to do with food, which she answered in a very matter-of-fact way. I could tell that she had concluded that even trying to talk me out of this would be a waste of her time, so she dropped any thought of doing so.

"So how do you do your injections?" she asked.

"Disposable syringes," I answered. At this, she sat back and said, "Oh well, there's something we need to change."

"I'm quite happy with the syringes, but I'm prepared to consider other options."

"Well," she said, "I advise that you go onto an insulin pump, but I get the feeling that you're going to resist that suggestion."

"Yes, I'm afraid I am," I said.

"Do you mind if I ask you why?"

"Not at all. For 34 years, I have been in total control of my existence. I manage my food, I manage my injections, I take responsibility for when something goes wrong and that's the way it needs to be. If I go over to using a pump, I'm giving up some of that control and responsibility to a machine and I can't have that. I can't rely on a machine to keep me alive, not when I've been doing it every minute of every day for the past

34 years, especially when I'm putting myself in danger over in the Sahara. I need to be in more control, not less."

"That's fair enough," she said. "Then I have another suggestion that I strongly encourage you to consider."

That was when she introduced me to the insulin pen.

"Hmmm, I've heard about these," I said.

"They've been around for quite some time now," said the doctor, rolling her eyes slightly. "This is how they work."

She then proceeded to go through the workings of what I had been resisting for many years. A lot of people had been recommending that I swap across from syringes to the pen, but I had been resisting. I had been working on the 'If it ain't broke, don't fix it' life philosophy.

She worked through the mechanics of the unit, the vial of insulin that it used and the various advantages that it had over the syringes. But it wasn't until she brought out one of the needles, screwed it on to the pen and then pulled off its cover that I was finally convinced. The needle was so fine; it was actually a little difficult to see. And the fact that each pen comes as a complete, self-contained kit was the final selling point. I was convinced.

So after 30-something years of using disposable syringes, I was finally convinced to modernise the next step. I had started all those years ago with the glass syringe and their tram track needles. They were cumbersome, would often stick as you pushed the plunger and rather painful. The needles were reusable and quickly became blunt. The whole process, while a lifesaver, was wrought with pain and ongoing management problems. I had progressed on to the disposable syringes after a couple of years. These were a vast improvement on the glass syringe but having hundreds or thousands of injections every year for decades resulted in growing problems, even with them. The fat under the skin gets hard and lumpy and becomes impossible to inject into. Also, the insulin can stop being absorbed, which of course then affects the ongoing management of the diabetes. So progressing to the pens and their ultra-fine needles would be a significant move.

Next on Donna's list of requirements was a visit to a sports nutritionist. I didn't rush off immediately to find one, really not being sure of how they would be able to help. I just continued on, week after week, with my ever more demanding training walks.

By now, it was late 2008 and I was walking 20 or 30 kilometres each weekend, often walking on both Saturday and Sunday. Plus I was leaving an hour early for the trip to work most days, getting off the train at an earlier station and walking into the city from there. All of this was taking a toll on my diabetes management, with my sugar levels sometimes swinging wildly. One morning, as I was walking to work, I was ducking across a busy road. This road is a main thoroughfare in Melbourne, carrying trucks around the city centre. As I was halfway across, judging the timing of the traffic lights at each end of the bridge I was on, I realised that my vision was wobbling and I could no longer clearly see what the traffic was doing. I was able to duck between two cars that were momentarily stopped in the traffic and get to the other side. I was rapidly losing control as a severe low-sugar episode swung into action. My legs were now starting to wobble and cave at the knees, so I took off my backpack and dug into my emergency food for a fruit juice box. That was enough to get me the last ten minutes of walk to the office, where I again dug into my emergency food.

Worryingly, that sort of situation was becoming more and more common. If it had been two minutes later when I was on that bridge, the chances are good that I would not have been able to judge the gaps in the traffic, or the speed of the oncoming vehicles, or have been able to see clearly enough to get through the line of traffic without being hit by another car or truck. Being killed crossing a road in peak-hour traffic was not why I was doing this, so something needed to be done. The situation I found myself in at this stage of the training, when I was only a quarter of the way towards the event, was only going to get much worse as I upped the distances and the times.

Meanwhile, with the increasing distances I was covering every weekend, I was starting to suffer foot problems. When I first noticed it, I considered that it was temporary and would fix itself. One day, I'll accept that magic like 'It will fix itself' rarely happens in the real world. I persevered for a few weeks until it became obvious that it was getting worse, not better, and this was when I was doing 50 kilometres per week, not 250.

I hunted out a sports podiatrist whose practice was close to work and made an appointment. Being a sports specialist, he wasn't overly surprised by a type 1 diabetic attempting to do the Marathon des Sables. Over the years, he had treated many people from the strange world of extreme sports.

His help was invaluable. He was able to show me on a model exactly where my foot pain was coming from and what was causing it. From his many years of treating runners, jumpers, sprinters and many other people wearing *lycra*, his understanding of the engineering of the foot was unquestioned. From my two, rather expensive, sessions with him, I was able to continue my training with the confidence that I knew how to manage the errant ligament that had been damaged in a childhood accident when I was eight years old. He showed me how to tape my foot to replace the job that the damaged ligament was unable to do.

In retrospect, my second visit to the podiatrist was a little bit cheeky on my part, although at the time I didn't think twice about it. Keep in mind that I was preparing for an event in the Sahara desert on the other side of the planet, where I would be isolated from normal civilisation for a week.

As soon as I had got home after the first visit, Donna and I carefully stripped off each piece of the strapping tape. We measured it and I made a diagram of where it had been on my foot. I then proceeded to tape and re-tape my foot numerous times, in order to learn how he had done it and to understand the purpose for each piece of the complex taping process. A few weeks later, after I had done numerous training walks and had gone through the taping process many times, I made another appointment with the podiatrist. My reason for the second appointment was to get his confirmation that my taping efforts were good enough and that I had correctly remembered the process. I figured out while I was there that his understanding for why I had made the second appointment was so he could tape my foot again. When I told him quite proudly that I had undone his taping and made diagrams of it, the look on his face told me everything. It was only at that moment that I realised that he saw his job as being my ongoing official taper.

Oops! I still haven't worked out how he expected me to tape my foot when I was in Morocco. Maybe he thought he would do it before I left Melbourne, and it would last all the way through until the end of the event. Oh well.

Meanwhile, normal life still continued. We still went shopping for groceries each week, went to work and drove the kids to their sporting events. Donna and I were also working on another part of our 'agreement', being to turn my extreme marathon effort into an exotic holiday for both of us.

The plan so far was that we would fly to England and spend a few days with Donna's sister in London. I would then fly to Morocco and join up with some of my tent mates in Marrakesh, from where we would travel to the meet up point of Ouarzazate (Wah_za_zat) to join the rest of the competitors managed by the Colorado agent. The original plan was that Donna and our friend Nick would, a few days later, fly to Marrakesh and then travel on to Ouarzazate, to be there when we all returned after the event. Everybody who knew me knew that I'd be a physical wreck, plus also facing potential medical difficulties. Managing type 1 diabetes during extended periods of exercise has an added complexity, in that the body uses up some, most or all of the natural store of glucose that is stored around the liver. Everybody has this storage, but the process of using and rebuilding it is automatic for people who don't have type 1 diabetes. For me, as my body automatically rebuilt the storage around the liver, it needed to use some of the carbohydrate that I was eating daily, meaning that there was less available hour by hour for my normal living requirements. Does it sound complicated? Once you understand it, it's not so complicated, but as none of the rebuilding can be controlled or managed, making allowances for it in the days after the event was going to be very tricky and potentially dangerous for me. The coach trip back to

Ouarzazate from the Sahara was going to take five hours, and I would need to still eat like I was doing the event. But once back at Ouarzazate and back to normal eating, I was going to need the safety of somebody to be with me.

After the reunion at Ouarzazate, the plan was then that the three of us would return to Marrakesh, spend a few days or a week, then all fly back to England and spend some time in The Lakes District with Nick.

Meanwhile, normal life in 2008 continued.

Murphy's Law

We went to IKEA one weekend to buy a bookshelf for Donna's work room at home. Donna loves IKEA. As she was helping me to load the bookshelf into the car for the drive home, she winced momentarily, then mentioned that she'd hurt herself slightly. She mentioned a couple of times on the 30-minute drive home that her back was hurting, but we both cast it off as being not really important. The next morning, however, it was starting to look like something serious may have happened.

Over the next few months, Donna went off to the doctor a number of times as her back was still hurting and seeming to get worse. The doctor was proscribing painkillers of increasing strength until she eventually advised that further investigation was needed and referred Donna to a specialist. As you read this, please remember that I'm compressing months of pain and anguish and doctors' visits down to a few sentences.

The specialist was concerned that there was some real damage, so gave Donna some ultrasounds, followed by injections directly into the spine. He had found that while Donna was helping to load the bookcase into the car, she had twisted slightly and caused one of those incidents that notoriously reduce a person to a life of pain. She had damaged one of the disks in her spine. Any wonder she was in so much constant pain!

As time progressed, so did Donna's pain. The injections didn't help and eventually the specialist was out of ideas. It's not a good thing when the back specialist has run out of ideas. Donna's GP was now getting concerned about the amount of painkillers she was on, as one of them was being referred to on TV as 'Hill Billy Heroin', and her dosage on that one was increasing week by week. She was now on a very strong dosage of that and a number of other life-altering drugs just so she could get through each day. This was starting to seem like an episode of Jerry Springer, but it was all genuine and easily explained. But that didn't ease the doctor's concerns.

Donna was now on the books for an operation on her back by a spinal surgeon at The Alfred Hospital. The original timing for the operation would have allowed Donna to still make the planned trip with a little bit of time to spare, but sadly it was delayed a number of times. Donna wasn't happy and neither was the GP. Neither was I. As you can imagine, there was a lot going on in our house by now, with me deeply involved in training and doing the preparations for my big walk, and Donna deeply involved with her back problems and trying to organise the rest of our holiday.

After a number of delays to the operation, it was with great regret from all involved that we decided that Donna was not going to be able to make the trip. This was not a decision taken lightly. There was so much going on in our house at that moment in history that this really became the only possible choice. It was either that, or give up on 22 months of training and around $5000 spent on preparations. The timing now was such that, even if Donna went in for her operation the next day, there was not enough time left for her expected recovery to enable her to make the trip. This was a gut-wrenching decision that would have to wait until 2012 before it could be rectified.

Why Can't You Increase It?

By early 2009, I'd reached the limit that my food choices could take me to. My training was now 60 or more kilometres per week and I was noticing some problems. My food choices were getting difficult to eat for hour after hour, becoming cloying and sickly. But also, I was finding that by the end of a long training walk, say 30 kilometres, I was simply out of energy. I'd stumble through the door a mere shell of a human. This was certainly not going to work non-stop in the Sahara. Something needed to be done.

After finding a specialist sports nutritionist on the internet, I went to speak to her, not holding out much hope for anything of great importance. It was one of Donna's conditions that I didn't skimp on doing what was necessary to do the event properly, so I swallowed my pride and went along.

Well, again I was shown how to eat crow. The young lady that greeted me was from South Africa and explained to me that she had worked with many athletes to fine tune their diet to maximise their ability. When I asked her about her understanding of type 1 diabetes, she explained that she had specialised in sports nutrition requirements for diabetics.

Now that we had clarified the ground rules, she went on to change my life. I know that's a big statement, but it's the reality of what she was able to teach me. She brought me to a new level of understanding of diabetes, exercise and nutrition that astounded me. Why hadn't I known this from the beginning? Donna and I have discussed that question many times since, and the only conclusion that we can come to is that the diabetes medical community must believe that average people wouldn't be able to successfully manage it.

At this point, I must stress that any person with diabetes reading this must not take my words as being true and correct. Before even considering changing anything, you must first consult your diabetes management team and discuss with them. Also I will not be giving details, as the potential consequences for anyone who did try to follow my advice are too serious for me to do so.

The sports nutrition lady described to me the way the body gets energy, and specifically from carbohydrate. Of course it's the carbohydrate that is the focus of diabetes. She told me the science of calories and grams of carbohydrate, then went on to ask me questions about the Marathon des Sables. She wanted to know how far I'd be walking each day, what the temperature would be in the Sahara, how much I weighed and how much my backpack would weigh. I really didn't understand the reason for all of these specific questions, but answered them anyway. She then pulled out a chart and showed me, based on the information that I'd given, how many calories my body would need to complete the distance each day. Then, given the science behind grams of carbohydrate and calories, how much carbohydrate I would need to eat each day to be able to walk the expected distances.

I was gob-smacked! She made it all look so straightforward and scientific. It was purely mathematics. I was speechless. Then she asked me what my intension was for my insulin. I told her that I intended reducing my insulin each day, obviously. That is the standard approach taken by a diabetic when they are doing some exercise. She asked why I was planning on reducing it, to which I answered that it was the standard way. She would know that surely. Then she said something that almost made me gulp. She said that rather than reducing the dosage, she was going to advise that I raise the dosage by a significant amount.

What? I couldn't believe what I was hearing.

I told her that I was very nervous about doing that and she agreed that she expected I would be. She must have heard that reaction previously when advising other diabetic sports people. To put it into simple words, she was advising me that I would use petrol to put out a fire instcad of water, and that it was safe to do so. Then she went on to explain how the exercise/insulin/carbohydrate process works in a way that nobody else had ever explained it. Putting it into my simple words, she explained that insulin was like the pipe down which the carbohydrate flows into the cells to provide energy. When the cells need more energy because of exercise, they need more carbohydrate. To get more carbohydrate to them, they need a bigger pipe. As insulin is the pipe, they need more insulin. So more exercise? Then more carbohydrate so more insulin.

This was the case when the exercise was of the endurance type. When exercise is of the sprinting type, or just one day, this approach is not necessarily the right one. But for extreme endurance events, this was the way it worked.

After 34 years of managing my diabetes, I was in awe of this young lady. She had simply opened the door to a whole new level of understanding for me. So much made sense now. I was able to think back to situations in the past and now understand how they had come about. If she happens to be reading this, thank you very much for educating me.

Marathon des Sables – Preparation – 2009

Training for an event like this, in essence, involves lots and lots of kilometres over lots and lots of training walks. There is nothing that can be done to substitute for many kilometres on the road. By April 2009, after 12 months of pretty full-on training and preparation, I was regularly walking a marathon on one day of a weekend, plus a shorter walk on the other day. This in addition to the ongoing walks to work most mornings of the week. To say that our family life was centred around my training would be to understate it considerably.

By now, I had overcome the problems I had discovered with my foot and overcome the issues surrounding the food I was going to be eating during the event. I had found food that was loaded with carbohydrate, was light, self-contained and packaged in such a way that made it easy to carry and tough, so it could withstand the rigors of the desert. I still had to determine the food that I would be eating in the morning before each day's walking and in the evening after each day's walk.

I also had the extra consideration of the long stage of the event, which was a distance of between 85 and 90 kilometres. This stage was non-stop for that distance, so was going to take me at least 24 hours and possibly as much as 36. So I needed to have food that would get me through that period without jeopardising my health and safety. I couldn't just eat the 'walking food' for that whole period; I would also need something more substantial during that period. But that was a decision for the future. Meanwhile, I pushed on into the unknown territory of endurance.

Wilsons Prom 2009

In my humble opinion, one of God's gardens is the Wilsons Promontory National Park in Victoria. This park of 125,000 acres, 220 kilometres south east of Melbourne, was rescued from the ravages of mining before too much damage could be done. After much thinking, planning and plotting, I decided that Wilsons Prom could become part of my training. There are a number of rugged walking tracks around The Prom, with a loose network of tracks in the southern prom leading to the lighthouse. The lighthouse is near the southernmost point of mainland Australia but can only be approached either on foot after a long and arduous hike from Tidal River, or by boat with the threat of being dashed against the rocks of this forbidding piece of coast. It had always been a desire of mine to walk to the lighthouse, but now I had a real reason to do so. Plus now I'd been training for 12 months, so was more likely to be able to make the trek.

After making inquiries and getting all the maps I could find, I learnt the track does a loop south along the west coast from Tidal River, then Oberon Bay, then down to the lighthouse, on up the east coast of the prom through Waterloo Bay, Refuge Cove and Sealers Cove, then back to Tidal River, a total distance of between 55 and 60 kilometres. After 12 months of training, I considered that I was now ready to tackle that challenge.

The original plan for my inaugural Wilsons Prom walk was to practice for the 90 kilometre non-stop leg of the Marathon des Sables by first doing the Lighthouse loop of around 55 kilometres, followed immediately by a 40 kilometre lesser-loop track. The downright humour of that concept was yet to strike me.

After much consideration, planning, working through 'what-if' situations, determining my potential food requirements and then multiplying them by one and a half, I considered I was ready. It was May 2009 and I set off for The Prom, as it is affectionately known in Victoria. Was I ready for this? Well, in the last 12 months, I had covered over 2000 kilometres of slogging up and down hilly, gravel roads with an ever-increasing weight on my back, hiking along in all weather conditions except snow. I had walked through sunup into rain and completed marathons in the hail. I had never stopped and never given up. Yes, I considered I was ready for this.

I was wrong.

But before we jump to that conclusion, let's get there in a step-by-step process that will open to you the humour behind my thinking. After leaving Melbourne and taking a couple of hours to drive to The Prom, everything was going according to plan. I left Tidal River on time, at five o'clock in the morning, and walked in the dark south along the beach with my headlamp on. It was a bit eerie being in the dark but hearing the surf crashing on my right. Everything went according to plan and I found myself at Oberon Bay on time and feeling OK.

By the time I was at the lighthouse, I was a little bit behind schedule. It had taken maybe an hour or so longer than I had anticipated to get there, but as this was my first visit to the lighthouse, I was thrilled just to be there. I had a rest, filled up my water, then continued on. So far I had completed about 20 kilometres of the planned 90 or more.

Forty minutes after leaving the lighthouse, I came on a long, long uphill struggle which, by the time I got to the top, had my legs wobbling. I had felt this in the past with one stretch of the Oxfam Trailwalker. It too was a long uphill struggle and had caused similar difficulty. I pushed on up in some considerable discomfort, eventually getting to the top. Down the other side and on to Waterloo Bay was quite easy, but now I was some hours behind schedule. I was also starting to consider that the full double loop that I had originally planned may not be feasible. This became more apparent when I got to the end of Oberon Bay and was struggling along a wonky stretch of boardwalk. By now, it was 4:30 and my original plan had me almost back to Tidal River by now. And yet here I was only just over halfway along on the first loop, with the sun soon to go down. This wasn't looking good.

The marathon distance of 42 kilometres came and went with me now in considerable difficulty. Here I was in the middle of nowhere. It was pitch-black at ten o'clock at night and my body was simply out of energy… or so I thought. My legs were shaking with the relentless up and down and bumping of the rough track… or so I thought. I was so exhausted that I was losing my balance on slippery rocks and getting an agonising stream of leg cramps. This was no longer fun and I wasn't enjoying myself. Oh, and to make sure that the picture was complete, it was now starting to rain lightly.

In my exhausted state my brain wasn't working at 100%, so when confronted with a rocky area at the top of a hill, with an unclear track, I was unable to clearly determine the correct way forward. I tried numerous times to find which way the track went, even backtracking and then making another approach, to see if the direction suddenly became apparent. Sadly that didn't happen. I knew that I was exhausted and therefore it was likely that my sugar was low. I also knew that I was close to the edge of a cliff, as I could hear the crashing of the waves way down below. With this combination of conditions, being exhausted, not thinking clearly and effectively lost, I decided to stop right there and sleep on the rock under the large poncho I was carrying.

Miraculously, the rest of that night went without drama. Sure I was exceedingly cold and uncomfortable, hunched as I was under a poncho on the top of a huge rock, but I had managed to survive the cold and light rain and was clear headed when dawn finally arrived. If anyone had seen me, it would have looked comical as light rain was still falling as I was trying to have my morning injections. So now I was sitting on a rock, under a poncho, fumbling around with my insulin pens trying to keep everything clean, dry and in order as I injected myself.

Another consideration at that moment was that Donna had no idea where I was or if I was still alive. Mobile telephone reception at Wilsons Prom in 2009 was rudimentary, so I hadn't been in contact with her since three o'clock the previous afternoon. I was starting to imagine what she could be thinking and what she might be doing, but on that rock in the early morning light I was powerless to do anything about that. All I could do was get myself together and move towards Tidal River until I eventually found some signal.

Three hours later, after a long haul of climbing and slipping in the muddy conditions, my mobile phone suddenly sprang to life. It was now over 18 hours since I had the last reception and people were getting concerned. As soon as the phone beeped the first time, I stopped where I was to avoid losing that pocket of signal. Message after message came flooding in from Donna, from one of my brothers and my daughters, all of them gravely concerned for my safety. By now, my ancient phone was running short of battery, so I messaged Donna to tell her I was OK and asked her to pass the message on. Not wanting to become like the boy who cried wolf, I wanted to allay people's concerns so they had some left if ever I really needed it.

Once back in the comfort and safety of home, I winced at how this inaugural Lighthouse Loop had turned into a black comedy of errors. I struggled to believe how misguided my thinking had been and vowed to learn from the many mistakes. Not only did my original plan have me completing the big loop within 12 to 14 hours, which on the gravel roads around our house was certainly possible, but it also had me then completing a second but smaller loop in the next eight to ten hours. I was kidding myself to the extreme. It finally took me around 30 hours to finish the first loop, and I could have died in the process. Sure I learnt a lot along the way, but my misguided thinking was a real slap in the face. That had to become an important, if severe, lesson.

Four weeks later, I was off to do it again, only this time changing many aspects of the plan from the first failure. Plus I was four-weeks fitter. These Wilsons Prom adventures were only the icing on a very large cake of training day after day after day. By now, I was walking 60 to 70 kilometres each week and often doing a full marathon on one day of the weekend. It wasn't until a couple of years later, when thinking back to this time, that I realised just how fit I had been in 2009. The strange part about it though was that I was constantly so exhausted and tired that I felt like the walking dead, rather than a honed athlete ready to take on the Sahara.

Many aspects of this second attempt remained the same as the first. I still left from Tidal River at the same time of day, heading in an anti-clockwise direction. But this time I had totally discarded any foolish notion of doing a second loop, being satisfied to simply finish the 60 kilometre main loop non-stop. That was my goal for this second attempt.

Well, it didn't happen. But I did at least get further than the first time before having to stop. This time I had brought an alarm clock with me, so I could have confidence of waking up if I needed to stop along the way. And the alarm clock came in useful, if not maybe for the reason it was intended.

Being more aware now of what the conditions were like, I was able to make much better progress. It was still late afternoon daylight as I passed over the top of the rock that I had slept on the previous time. With a shiver, I saw just how close I had been to the edge of the cliff that first time and was also able to see why finding the path down off the rock had been so difficult. I pushed on hard as the sun went down and the headlamp came out.

Walking along bush tracks with the headlamp is hard work, as the light from it is focused directly only on whatever is directly in front of you. It's a bit spooky, to be honest, until you get used to it and care is required when the ground is rocky. It would be far too easy to 'do an ankle' on a slippery rock or tree root, so progress is significantly reduced. This was a good lesson for the overnight section in the Sahara. The rocks there won't be slippery, but there are plenty of them and they can be rough and jagged.

Again I was a shell of a human being as I blundered into the Sealers Cove campsite at close to midnight. I was now working on autopilot, so considered that I could keep going, even though it was dark, cold, wet, miserable and still a long way to go. From Sealers Cove, there is an unforgiving climb from the beach, along a damp, muddy track, to the top of the saddle and I wasn't looking forward to that.

I thumped unceremoniously down the last bit of slope from the camp site to the water crossing. Anyone who happened to be camping at Sealers Cove that night would have thought that they were under attack from a Yeti or something. But I was stopped in my tracks when I got to the water's edge. I knew that there was a wet crossing and was prepared for it. At extreme low tide, you can be very lucky and wade through quickly with not much water getting into your boots, but for most of the time, this crossing was at least knee-deep and often much more severe.

This was one of those times.

When I got to the water's edge and turned my head to see where the water was, I had to stop and think for a moment. What was I looking at? I was expecting to see a strip of sand, then the water, then more sand about 30 metres beyond that. But instead I was seeing just water, right up to the small step down to the sand. The tide was up high, meaning that a water crossing would have me stripped off and holding all of my gear above my head, as I headed into the dark towards sand that I couldn't see because it was too far away, with water possibly up to my neck. All of this while wearing my headlamp and trying to keep it dry.

Obviously none of that was about to happen. I had been stopped in my tracks by a significant high tide and had no choice but to find a place to sleep until the tide went down. So I turned around and headed back in the direction of the camping ground, which was back up the narrow track, in amongst the trees and bush. There were a few tents scattered around, so I crept around as best I could so as not to disturb those campers currently snuggled in their sleeping bags. Fortunately for me, over the years the park rangers at Wilsons Prom have gradually improved facilities and Sealers Cove now sported a wooden toilet block with a small veranda forming a shelter from any rain. So, putting any pride I may have left in my back pocket, I laid down on the hard boards of the veranda right outside the toilet doors, set my clock for the morning and tried to get some sleep.

After a short while, maybe 30 minutes, maybe only five, I became aware that I wasn't thinking clearly. I should have been asleep by now, but instead my mind was racing in weird circles. Due to my current circumstances, it was clear to me that I needed to be hyper-vigilant as I was now into what I refer to as 'endurance mode'. My current circumstances were tough and likely to get tougher before I got back to civilisation, so when I recognised something odd happening with my head, I chose to assume the worst and have a fruit strip. As the effect of this started to kick in, it enabled me to realise just how bad my blood sugar level really was. It hadn't occurred to me when I had stumbled in to Sealers Cove, but it was now becoming clear that I was on the verge of a desperate situation.

I took out one of the sports gels from the food pocket in my trousers and squeezed that down my neck. Then I followed that with another fruit strip. I sat there on the hard boards of the veranda to consider how I now felt and decided that another sports gel was required, as these are easier to get down than the fruit strips and act much more quickly. All of this was telling me just how bad my BSL had been when I had arrived at the camp ground. After another fruit strip, washed down with some water, I was finally confident that I would see morning, so curled up on the hard boards and got some sleep.

The next morning, when the world looked a whole lot different in the bright morning sun, I pushed up the long hill from Sealers Cove, stopped to receive the anxious messages from Donna at the signal spot and then finally arrived back at Tidal River. When I called in to the rangers' office to let them know that I had returned, the lady behind the counter was interested in what I was doing. I told her about the Sahara and then about attempting the Lighthouse Loop. She told me that doing the loop was a well-known activity for those wanting to do something extreme, then asked me a strange question. She asked me which way I had gone around. I thought it odd that she should focus on that, but I told her that I'd gone anti-clockwise.

"Oh no, no, no," she said, "that's the wrong way. You need to go clockwise."

"Why?" I asked, intrigued that she should even have an opinion on the subject.

"Everyone who does the loop, and there's a few extreme people who do it, all know that anti-clockwise is much too hard. Clockwise is easier. For a start, you've got that hell of a climb after you leave the lighthouse…" Yes, I knew about that one.

"Then you've got the climb out of Sealers which, by that stage of your loop, is a real killer. No, the best way to do the loop is clockwise."

So now I knew. My two attempts so far had both been virtually doomed to failure from the start, even by the experts. Learning this so suddenly and succinctly both sagged my shoulders and gave me a boost. I no longer felt like I'd failed and was immediately looking forward to the next loop in a month's time. As Bullwinkle says to Rocky, "This time for sure."

A month later, I had managed to convince another fool, er… I mean adventurer, to do the loop with me. Robin from my work was a long-time bushwalker, although being from New Zealand, he was more correctly a tramper. It was great to have somebody else along facing the challenges with me.

These walks were not easy by any stretch, so to be able to share the experience also meant sharing expertise. One of the things that I had learnt by now was the importance of hydration supplements in the water, or electrolytes, or whatever you wish to call them. They all achieve the same purpose, no matter how you have them. Robin had never attempted anything quite as gruelling as this before and found at about the halfway mark that he was spent and was suggesting that he was going to take the shorter path back so as not to stop me from completing the loop. I could tell his condition by how he was looking. With some encouragement, and by showing him the package that they came in, I was able to coerce him to give them a try, so put two in his water bottle. These supplements act like magic and over the next ten minutes his mood and his physical condition picked up significantly. By the time we got to the spot where the tracks diverge, he was feeling good enough to continue towards the lighthouse. Still drinking the water with the supplements, by the time we got to the lighthouse, he admitted that he felt magnificent.

Robin never again suggested he was going to cut a loop walk short. Electrolytes are important. This was going to come back much into the future to haunt me.

Wilsons Prom Full On

Midway through 2009, my training had brought me to a point where I was starting to consider myself almost ready. Physically, I couldn't expect a lot more improvement. At 52 years of age, what I was achieving week after week was, to cast modesty to the side for a moment, quite amazing. I had never been an 'athlete', so had started this endeavour from a very basic starting point. I was now at a level where, with ten minutes warning, I could be on the road and walk a marathon with no problems at all, with enough food on my back to last a week.

With regards to the management of my diabetes, I had made enormous strides. I was now settled on the food to eat during a day of walking. I was fine tuning the food to eat at the start of the day and at the end of the day. I still had some decisions to make there, but the general approach was now decided. I had learnt about the need for electrolyte supplements and considered that subject now closed. I now had most of my final gear for the Sahara, with only some of the less important items to get. I did still need to get the sleeping bag but had already found that it wasn't going to be difficult to get that. So now I considered that almost all of my focus could now be devoted purely to training.

Three weeks out of four, I was now doing marathon distances combined with 20 or 25 kilometres on the other day of the weekend. When I thought back to where I started at, when five kilometres was comfortable and ten was a long way, I knew I really had come a long way. On the fourth weekend of each month, I was doing a Wilsons Prom lighthouse loop.

By now, I had become sophisticated enough that I was carrying a satellite tracker with me on my Wilsons Prom trips. I had recently learnt about these and had bought one and set it up so that anyone who had the web site could, at the click of a mouse, see where I was. I introduced these to the picture with a dual purpose. Firstly, it brought an extra level of safety and comfort when I was doing the lighthouse loops on my own, as Robin didn't always join me. The other was to fine tune how it worked for both myself and those who would be watching me progress across the Sahara. Modern technology is amazing. My team mate at work asked me one Monday after I had a done a loop, why I had stopped for about 20 minutes just after I had left Waterloo Bay. I was amazed. Yes, I had stopped and it was because it was halfway up the long climb out of Waterloo Bay and I was feeling tired. I sat down for a rest and dropped off to sleep for 20 minutes while sitting on a rock. He was also to ask me in the future, why I had turned off the tracker in Spain. But we'll get to that much later.

My performance on the loops was getting consistently better and better. So was Robin's. He didn't come on every walk, missing about every second one. But he was there to share some memorable experiences. There was the time we were crossing over the low point to the lighthouse right at the moment that a thundery squall struck. For around 90 seconds, we were pounded by howling winds, thunder and lightning and general mayhem, dramatic enough that I nearly lost my poncho and backpack. We had to grab on to each other and help each other across to where we could shelter in rocks. Of course that was just in time for the squall to blow itself out.

Then there was the time that Robin, who was walking behind me, suddenly gave a shout of shock.

"Didn't you see that?" he asked.

"See what?" I asked.

"The snake. You stepped over a snake!"

There was the time we were climbing out of Sealers Cove, heading for Refuge Cove. The weather was glorious sunshine and we were in high spirits. Suddenly we heard a sound coming from behind us and turned to see what it was.

We couldn't see anything until Robin pointed to the middle of the bay and yelled, "Look! It's a whale!" We stood there for the next ten minutes watching a whale blow through its blow hole, lift its enormous side flipper into the air and slap it down on the water surface with the sound of a cannon and generally make us glad to be alive and here to see it. Robin was like an excited, little boy for the rest of the day after that. He loves all creatures great and small, which is why he nearly fainted with joy one night when we were just stepping down onto Norman Bay beach, just 30 minutes from the finish of our loop, when we were confronted in the light of our headlamps with a wombat, standing right in the middle of our path. We stood there and waited as it slowly waddled out of the way and we could keep going.

Robin was also with me the night that, at the 50-kilometre point of the loop, I started to feel quite strange. We'd been pushing along that day and, as we were on the fire track near Roaring Meg, I started to lose control of my legs. I was already suffering painful cramps, which was a regular aspect of these walks for me, but this time they got worse until I was having trouble walking. Finally, with great regret, I sat down on the track to give the cramps a chance to go away. I was feeling exhausted and Robin was a little concerned. So was I, to be honest. Understandably, I considered that my sugar might be going low, so I had an extra fruit strip and sports gel, but they didn't seem to help. Eventually we got going again and I struggled along until we got to Halfway Hut, where we chose to have another good rest. I was worried about what might be going on, so I reluctantly agreed with Robin's suggestion that we stay there in the hut for the rest of the night.

I was to learn later that this was a flashing, screaming warning light, yelling at me that there was a problem. All I could think of was a sugar problem, maybe combined with exhaustion, so I pushed it aside. Oh, how I wish I had taken more notice!

Murphy's Law
Revisited

Finally, it all got too much for Donna, who was living with immense pain every minute of every day. She called the hospital to find out the latest status for her operation and started crying as she spoke with one of the senior admin people. Fortunately, he was one of those 'can-do' people who went to work to actually help people, not just shuffle papers, and started asking questions. He was able to determine that Donna's case had indeed fallen between the cracks and her operation should have happened months previously. As a result, he organised not only for Donna to go to the top of the list, but also that she would be given the preeminent spinal doctor in all of Melbourne.

La Grande Adventure –
Getting There

After two years of hard work, training, planning and organising, I would have hoped that the last couple of weeks before leaving would have been calm. But alas, that was not the case. Almost right up to the moment of departure tickets were being printed, passports were being checked, final arrangements being made. Not least amongst this was the all essential backpack. The first 'final' packing of that was two weeks prior to departure. The final 'final' packing was the afternoon before departure. But at least, as I was to work out later, I didn't forget anything.

At last, it was time to leave for the airport. It would have been nice if I was calm by this stage but alas, this was not to be. I was stressed and tense and just eager to be on the plane. Our friend Karen, who was going to prove to be a great help for Donna over the next few weeks, arrived early to pick us up and drive us. All of my family, brothers, mother and assorted others, were there to say goodbye, so it was a loud and jumbled farewell.

I wish I could say that the flight to London was boring, but unfortunately a small drama happened on the way. The flight to Doha was quite normal and comfortable, as was the connecting flight to London, up to the point that I asked for an orange juice. When I took my first sip of the juice, I thought that maybe I'd been given mango juice instead. It tasted a little odd. I took another small taste and then I realised that something was definitely wrong. I mentioned to the hostess that there was something wrong with the juice and she went away to get a fresh one for me. Meanwhile, my mouth started to tingle and I could feel a strange sensation in my mouth and throat.

Suddenly, four hostesses came rushing up the aisle and asked me if I was OK. They urgently gave me an ice-cream, a fruit juice in a box and a bottle of water and were showing great concern about my welfare, which I found odd and strangely perplexing. My mouth was definitely feeling odd and now I had a sickening taste of chemicals in my mouth, throat, nose and sinuses.

The poor hostess, who I felt very sorry for, confirmed what had happened. The dishwasher used to clean the glasses had only been through half its cycle, leaving the glasses covered in the cleaning solution rather than being rinsed clean. And now all I could taste and smell was the nauseating effect of chemicals. This was to last until the next day in London before it finally went away. The rest of the trip to London went without any further dramas, luckily, leaving me standing out in the public area of Heathrow a few minutes early, waiting for my ride. Tina, my sister-in-law who lives in London with her husband Ken, had been caught in traffic and was a little late arriving to pick me up. By the time she arrived, I had created visions of me being stranded at Heathrow airport as night fell, not knowing where I was meant to be going. However, they finally arrived and all was fine.

London—what can I say? There is something about London, and England in general, that makes Donna and I go a little funny. This was now my third trip to London, but I was still over-awed to be there. Donna and I have tried to work out what makes us go all mushy about being in London, and the best we can come to is some mystical sort of tribal memory. It's either that or simply that Donna and I are just repressed Anglophiles. Who knows, but I now had that mushy feel again.

Over the next three days, as I played with my backpack and other luggage, and as the details of the Ryanair flight to Marrakesh started to become clearer through talking with Tina, it became apparent that a major rethink of my luggage requirements was in order. Having never flown with joyful airlines like Ryanair or Easy Jet before, I wasn't until then aware that they make their money by charging for absolutely everything. If my booked in luggage was even a few hundred grams over the 15 kg that Tina had arranged for, it was going to cost me substantial amounts of money. And as this trip was already costing a lot of money, this was a 'joy' that I could well do without.

So I packed and unpacked, packed again and then repacked. I tried nearly every combination of checked in and cabin luggage I could think of, eventually finding the right combination of what goes where and what to discard and leave behind. This meant that my race backpack needed to have some contents transferred across to my cabin luggage bag and the race backpack became my booked in luggage. It also meant that I needed something lightweight to protect my backpack from damage. As I sat there in London, the most important thing in my field-of-view at that moment in time was my backpack.

The next day, I took myself off to the centre of London on the tube. I simply cannot go to London and not spend at least one day wandering around the city, travelling on the tube, seeing Buck House, etc. My goals for the day were to find something that would protect my backpack as it travelled to Marrakesh and to see some of the famous sites of London. The first was achieved with a visit to an outdoor shop in Oxford St. There I found a tough, adaptable and lightweight bag that I could use, so that job was now half complete.

As I was walking up Oxford St, calling into Marks and Spencer to browse around and be astounded at the range and quality of the food available for lunch down in the basement, I experienced the first bout of low sugar since leaving Melbourne. As I had left Melbourne 36 or 48 hours ago, I'd lost count, I was actually doing quite well. It was not far off lunch time and it quickly became obvious that I didn't have time to buy lunch to get rid of the low. With rapidly diminishing options, I stopped and pulled out a packet of emergency biscuits from my backpack. The sugar was dropping rapidly, so I ate quite a lot of biscuits to catch it and bring it back up. Even though this was the first low I had experienced since leaving home, I wasn't happy that it had happened. Here I was on my own in the centre of London. A major low was not a good idea.

The rest of the day was filled with activities that are, in my opinion, a must for anyone visiting London infrequently. These included a walk from Leicester Square down to Buck House past Nelson's Column, around St James Park, up through some amazing buildings with beautiful architecture, past 10 Downing St, back up to Trafalgar Square, where I then sat and watched all the people for a while, then back to Leicester Square and the tube back to Tina's place. In Paris, you visit the Eiffel Tower. In London, you visit these places.

The next day, Tuesday the 30th of March, was the last day in London before I left for Morocco. A visit to Harrods was a great way to see another side of London and an opportunity to buy a few small presents for the family. Over the years, Donna has accumulated a number of bags from Harrods, and now she had one more. While there, Tina and I got talking to a nice couple who were amazed by what I was about to do in the Sahara. The fellow was himself a type 1 diabetic, so he understood the danger I was facing and the difficulties I had been working with through the training and the event itself. It is conversations such as this which make all of the hard work seem more worthwhile.

Finally, it was Wednesday the 31st of March and the day to leave London and fly to Marrakesh. This was the start of a whole new challenge. I was leaving the relative safety and comfort of London and travelling to a new and exotic country, a city I'd never been to before but had grown up with songs on the radio about. And not only that but I was starting an extreme adventure. Was I nervous? Me? What do you think?

Ken drove me down the M-whatever motorway to Luton airport, getting me there only half an hour before departure time. Having never been to Luton before, I found it to be a cavernous building simply full of people, all lined up for their various flights. I eventually found the Ryanair queue for Morocco at the farthest end of the building and rushed to join it, only to discover it was moving at a rate that would have us all booked in by around midday. As the plane left at 5:25 a.m., less than half an hour away, that could have been a problem.

And so it was. With a lot of hand wringing on my part, and shuffling from foot to foot, I finally got booked in five minutes AFTER the plane was scheduled to leave. With a smile on her face, the girl behind the counter suggested to me very politely that the plane was waiting to leave. "So I'd hurry if I was you." After running for what seemed like forever to the departure gate with my bags, and risking tripping and breaking my neck, they closed the door as soon as I was on the plane. Then Ryanair, in all their audacious ingenuity, offered to sell me a beer so I could get my breath back after running to the departure gate. That's what the bright and sparky recorded Irish voice said over the PA. The rotten mongrels had it all planned.

I will never fly with Ryanair again if I can avoid it.

La Grande Adventure – Getting There – Marrakesh

The old Marrakesh, or 'The Medina' as it is known, is simply an extraordinary place. I was to learn much later that the further out from the centre of Marrakesh that you travel, the more modern the city becomes. But the heart of Marrakesh, both geographically and spiritually, is the Medina. I had stepped back a hundred years in time.

After navigating through the maze of backstreets and alleyways that surround the Medina, the driver finally had me at my accommodation. As always in a new city, the first thing I had to do was to find a reliable source of food. It may sound too mundane for normal people, but uppermost in the mind of a type 1 diabetic is knowing where and how to get food. After 36 years, for me this was paramount. The charming lady looking after the villa, who spoke only French and Arabic, was nice enough to arrange for a taxi to come to pick me up and drive me to a 'supermarket'. The driver, who's English was less than my Arabic, was a charming little fellow who was only too pleased to help. The villa lady had explained to him that I needed a supermarket, so there was little drama explaining that to him. Between us we were able to use four languages to communicate—French, Arabic, English and hand signals.

The supermarket he took me to was old but quite large. It was similar to large old grocery stores in country towns in Saudi Arabia. An interesting thing that I discovered as I looked for breakfast food, fruit juice, milk and anything else that was durable, gluten-free and carbohydrate, was that the only recognisable brands were Coca Cola and Pepsi. Everything else was either a local brand or French. I did find a box of breakfast food which, with careful study of the eight languages presented on the side, I was able to determine was gluten free. That was definitely a 'phew' moment. At least now I had food to get me through the next few days of adventure.

After driving me around for over an hour to banks and supermarkets, as well as walking with me through the supermarket to carry my grocery basket, it came time to pay the driver. No matter which country you are in the world that doesn't speak English, this is always an interesting time. It is also one of those moments where you can get a snapshot of the integrity of the local people. Was he going to attempt to fleece me? After a little hand-wringing and nervousness, the driver finally told me that the fare was 100 dirhams. A quick division by seven told me that this was not a lot of Australian dollars and would have cost considerably more if we were in Melbourne. So I handed him the 100 dirhams and then gave him 20 more.

Within the walls of the old city of Marrakesh is a rabbit warren of little laneways that criss-cross and weave their way this way and that. It is truly amazing to see. After settling in to my room at the villa, I went for a walk to explore this amazing place. I was suddenly in the old Middle East, with donkey's and rugs and street markets and mosques and little motor scooters squirting blue smoke. It was enchanting and I wandered around, carefully so as not to get lost. I immersed myself in the humdrum for an hour before finally heading back to the villa to wait for Erick, one of the two MdS (Marathon des Sables) tent mates I had arranged to meet at the villa for the ride the next day to Ouarzazate.

Erick arrived at the allotted time, after being picked up from the airport. He came rolling in like a clap of thunder, so let me explain Erick to you.

Imagine, if you will, a very tall (six foot, five inches), proportionally large, very fit, very American, loud-speaking fellow who works as a project engineer with Microsoft. Now add to that image that he is a self-confessed geek who has managed to do a lot of things during his 40-something years of life, and you are starting to get a picture of Erick. Erick is larger than life and is a robustly charming fellow who was to become one of the focal points within tent 126.

Erick and I spent the rest of the afternoon and evening talking about our preparations for the MdS, our history, or lack of, with events such as this and our common interest in computer stuff. But I must say that on all of these subjects, Erick was able to trump me, and he wasn't even trying. The only subject where I was able to more than hold my own was that of diabetes.

The next day, Thursday the 1st of April, April Fool's day, found Erick, myself and the third member of the merry trio, Samantha from Canada, in a taxi on our way to Ouarzazate. This interestingly spelled town is a five-hour ride from Marrakesh through the Atlas Mountains. It seems to be a common thing to hire a taxi to travel from Marrakesh along this beautifully scenic and occasionally scary mountain road. I felt a bit like Harrison Ford or Matt Damon as we drove around the mountain passes and through villages big and small. Everywhere I looked, and I was trying to look everywhere, there were donkeys and mules and interesting-looking people going about their normal business.

When we arrived in Ouarzazate, the driver pulled into a car park that had many taxis and their drivers. As we were now hundreds of kilometres from Marrakesh, the problem was that our driver didn't know how to find our hotel. So after chatting with the other drivers for a few minutes, with us sitting in the idling Mercedes wondering what was going on, Erick was suddenly asked to squeeze into the back seat so another driver could climb into the front passenger seat. He was going to guide our driver to the hotel, apparently. Our momentary concern, with thoughts such as, "What the hell is going on?" was based on nothing more than the willingness of Moroccans to help one another.

It turned out that, purely by dumb luck, the hotel we were booked into was the same hotel that the rest of the American/Canadian/Australian/New Zealand contingent was going to be based in. Erick and I had been billeted together, so I would be enjoying the larger-than-life camaraderie and companionship of Erick for another night.

Once settled into the room, and after a brief explore around the grounds of the hotel, I went for the virtually mandatory walk to find a supermarket. There I was able to buy my bag of emergency food needed to cover that evening, the next morning and the five-hour coach trip to the Sahara the next day.

For non-diabetics reading this story, these 'bags of emergency food' are a vital requirement whenever a ready source of food, specifically carbohydrate, cannot be guaranteed. And when travelling, or in a new town or hotel, this can often be the case. Without the 'just-in-case' food, a diabetic faces the real risk of winding up in emergency in hospital, or even dying. I wish I was exaggerating, but sadly I'm not.

The next morning, at long last, things were starting to really happen. After the normal morning ablutions, we all gathered down in the reception area to be processed on to the coaches that were taking us out to the desert. This was the next phase of the trip into the unknown. We were told that the journey would take approximately five hours and that we would be provided with a packed lunch along the way. That was the full extent of our information as we all made our way onto the modern and comfortable coaches.

Everyone was in varying states of bewilderment and befuddlement. There were the experienced ones, for whom this was not the first MdS, who arranged themselves comfortably and sat there in relative serenity. Then there were the newbies, like me, who were caught in a whirlpool of excitement, concern and confusion. As we drove along, we didn't know which way to look. Did we look out of the windows on the left side to see the small fields of agriculture that were there, complete with their donkeys and men ploughing the fields, or did we look out of the right side windows to watch the development of the Sahara desert as it stretched away to the horizon? Or maybe we needed to meet, greet and talk to every person on the bus, find out where they came from and ask what was behind them being here. There was so much to do and so little time to do it.

After we had all piled on, organised our bags and stuff into the overhead racks and finally sat down, I was sitting next to a fellow from New York. I'm bad with remembering people's names, so unfortunately I can't remember his, but he was an IT manager for an international bank with his office in downtown Manhattan. I have to be honest here and tell you that I've never met anyone from 'downtown Manhattan' before, so even talking to this fellow had a spark of excitement for me. He was great to talk to and swap IT stories with, and proved to be a good friend much later in the story.

At long last, after five hours of diminishing villages and growing desert scenery, we arrived at the embarkation point for the final brief, bumpy ride to the first bivouac.

There was a small fleet of ex-military trucks waiting for us. This was starting to look serious and was taking on an air of urgency. It had taken so long, so much work, so much pain, and here I was about to drive into the Sahara desert.

We grabbed our luggage, which still consisted of our precious backpacks and our small suitcase for after the event, and made our way over to the waiting trucks. With our two pieces of luggage, the climb up onto the back of the trucks was not easy. I was fearful that my backpack was going to be damaged because for that to happen at this juncture would be tantamount to disaster. But everyone was careful and was each gripping their backpacks closely, so no damage was forthcoming. There wasn't much conversation during the short trip, bouncing a kilometre across the rocky track. Everyone must have been in a similar state of excited/

bewildered/ exhausted state of mind to myself, as the old trucks delivered us to our sanctuary for the next week.

Fortunately, Erick and I were able to find tent #126 easily, only about ten tents from the opening to the huge circle of tents that had been constructed. With over a thousand competitors and eight per tent, there were around 120 tents arranged in a giant circle. Each tent consisted of a large and very heavy canopy of black woven material that felt like it was made from woven camel hair. This was held up with sticks forming a tent shape, under which eight people could sit or sleep with a bit of a squeeze. On the stony ground were spread two rugs, each of which was the sleeping space for four people and their gear. It was cosy, but with some organising and compromise, quite enough room for the eight tent mates. These tents became our new home for the next eight days.

As the fleet of trucks gradually brought everyone from the coaches to the bivouac, our tent started to fill up. Erick, Sam and I already knew each other, so the new people for us were Stuart, Mark, Greg, Roz and Meghan. Stuart was a Scotsman who lives in Melbourne, Mark: an Englishman who just happened to live five kilometres up the road from where I live in Melbourne, Greg: an American who lived in… um… the USA, Roz: a young Australia girl/lady who lived in Sydney and Meghan was an American lady who lived near Yellowstone National park. So our tent had four Australians, three Americans and one Canadian. From the start, it felt like everyone was going to get along well.

Eventually, all had arrived and had introduced themselves, then settled down to play with their packs and gear. This was a fun game that we had all become addicted to as we trained and prepared for the MdS. The process of comparing gear and discussing the details of food choices filled a happy hour of discussion. I came to learn that we are very restricted in Australia with our choices of lightweight gear and ultra-marathon food. I took the opportunity to explain to everyone that I was a little different, which has become quite a common thing for me to tell people, and explained to them briefly why. Sam, being the GP from Canada, helped me to explain that I may act strangely at some point over the next seven days, and why, but that it was my responsibility to ensure that it didn't happen. Nobody had any questions, which is the usual response I get, which usually means that nobody had any previous exposure to diabetes and didn't want to look silly asking the wrong question, emphasising to me the importance of making sure I kept my sugar under control.

The rest of the afternoon was taken up with the getting-to-know-you activities and learning more about the arrangement of the bivouac. We found the toilets, the communication tent where emails and phone calls could be made, the administration tent and the food tent. This last one was important for us only for the first two nights and breakfast the next day.

The final activity for the day before we all settled down for our first night under the stars in the Sahara was for all 1026 of us to go to the food tent to get dinner. As there was no guarantee that the food would be OK for me, I was already self-sufficient, having eaten a freeze-dried meal before we went to the food tent. Self-sufficiency started for everyone else on the morning of the first day of the event and extended for six days plus one morning. Because of my food requirements and limitations, for me self-sufficiency started two days before the event and extended for an extra day at the end.

With a climbing level of excitement and expectation, after our first night sleeping in a Berber tent, we woke for the last day before the event began. This was the 'check-in' day, where the event officials work through quite an extensive checklist for every entrant, to ensure that everything is in order. This list included personal details, ECG results, backpack weight, weight of food, a check of compulsory gear, how many calories each competitor was carrying, race number, electronic monitor and emergency flare. All of this was quite straight forward and progressed well for me until it got to the checking of the ECG results. I had forgotten the advice that anyone over the age of 45 should have a stress ECG test. The two French doctors were quite concerned that I had only the results of a resting ECG. Strangely, this had nothing to do with my diabetes, so when I realised that it wasn't the diabetes that had them concerned, I laughed and joked with them and told them that I was healthier than anyone they were going to be seeing that day. Eventually, they smiled and agreed with me. Fortunately, common sense prevailed and they provided the required tick on the checklist.

The whole exercise was undertaken in French, with a smattering of English words and lots of hand signals.

The checking of the food and calories was interesting. The thing that concerned them most was the weight of my pack. At 15.2 kg, they were very concerned that this was too much. I found this odd, as the rules say that the pack can be up to 15 kg in weight. Yes, mine was over this limit by 200 grams, but that wasn't what concerned them. They were concerned because it weighed more than 14 kg. I found this a little strange but would eventually understand their concern.

As I was starting to get a bit concerned that they may not let me continue, which was within their rights to do so, I emphasised to them in my extremely poor French, slow, deliberate English and frantic waving of hands that I was walking, not running, and that I was diabetic and my food requirements were different to everybody else. This touched a nerve with the doctors. I could see them briefly discuss me amongst themselves and heard mention of diabetes a number of times. It appeared that they agreed between them that my diabetes changed things, so they accepted the weight of my pack and the amount of food I needed to carry. Many or most of the doctors associated with this event in the field were volunteers. I was told by many people that French doctors are considered some of the best in the world, so their concerns weren't to make life hard for me. They were attempting to stop me, or any of the other competitors, from killing ourselves. The conditions we would be facing from the next morning were going to be extreme.

At last, I received all of the required ticks and was now officially a participant in the 2010 running of the Marathon des Sables. An interesting side effect of the food weight thing was that the rules say that each person must carry a set minimum number of calories for each day. With the food that I needed to carry because of the carbohydrate requirements, I was carrying almost twice the minimum number of calories. No wonder people wonder why I'm as thin as I am.

There were now no more obstacles between myself and the event. The long road that began two years previously had now reached its end. All that was left to do now was to complete the 250 kilometres.

Back at the tent, everyone was in a mild state of euphoria, as everyone in our tent had now completed the check-in process. For the experienced competitors this meant slowly slipping into race mode. I could see them again fine tuning their packs, fine tuning protective strapping on their feet, shoulders and back, fine tuning the various items that they knew they would be needing over the next seven days. For the newbies, finishing the check-in process meant the great unknown was looming as the nerves stepped up a notch. Some of the newbies started to get advice on packing minutia from the experienced ones, suddenly deciding to cut two centimetres off a loose strap on their pack to save a gram, or looking forlornly at their choice of morning breakfast powder. After two years of intense hard work, I chose to have faith in what I had learnt about my pack and food and not change anything. I was aware of the danger of suddenly doubting what had taken two years to learn and making a mistake by ditching a packet of food or rearranging a vital strap on the pack. I saw at least one example where somebody had panicked and cut two centimetres off a strap, only to discover the next morning that the strap was now too short.

As all of this joyful fun was taking place, the lady who seemed to be Patrick Bowers right-hand man and English translator came by to have a chat with the tent. Very sadly, I don't remember her name, as she was a very nice lady whom I was to have dealings with throughout the event. She and I got talking and she was amazed by my story, being the diabetes, the two years of training, the intense focus on the food and the risk that I was running just being here. She told me that the media would likely want to have a talk with me later in the event. This was something that I was hopeful for, because it would have given me an opportunity to tell other type 1 diabetics that they don't have to give up on life just because of their illness. Sadly, it didn't happen, but we'll get to that in good time.

That evening, as I set about to warm water to cook my freeze dried meal, I discovered a couple of things. One was that in my desperate ditching of stuff in London to save weight in my luggage, I had inadvertently left the cigarette lighter behind. I'm not a smoker, but this was a mandatory piece of equipment, and I considered myself lucky that they hadn't bothered to check the contents of my bag of emergency gear during check-in. I also discovered that lighting the solid fuel block for the stove was not easy when there was even a slight breeze blowing, as there was this night.

I borrowed a cigarette lighter and then crouched in the lee of a scraggly bush in a desperate attempt to light my stove and heat the water. A lady came by looking for a spot to do precisely the same thing, so the two of us must have looked comical crouching down and desperately trying to get the little fuel tablet to burn. We eventually succeeded, so barely lukewarm water was eventually there for the food. But this was an experience I was going to call on again in 24 hours.

For the last time before the race started the next morning, dinner was provided for everyone at the dinner tent. But this time I knew that it wouldn't have much for me, so went along mainly for the socialising aspect. Everyone in the camp was in a hyped-up, up-beat mood that night, as everyone was trained up, paid up, revved up and eager to get going. After dinner, we all wandered back to our tents and bedded down for the night. I arranged my lightweight sleeping mat as best I could so that my knees and shoulders received whatever meagre benefit it would provide. As I lay down for the night in no mood to sleep, I discovered every rock, stone, unfortunate undulation and stone chip that lay under the rug on the ground. Sleeping hard on the ground is not comfortable, but it is do-able.

La Grande Adventure

Here it was, the first real day of the event. After nervously preparing our packs, checking food supplies and water, ensuring pockets contained the pre-planned contents, we were now standing at the start line. We had been instructed to be here a full 30 minutes before the start time as the organisers, i.e., Patrick Bower, took this opportunity each day to provide housekeeping updates and chest-pumping encouragement. That second part wasn't necessary today. As there was so much adrenalin coursing through the competitors, he would have been wasting his time. But he did anyway. Today the housekeeping consisted mainly of general statements, such as: "Drink all of your water," "Don't forget your salt tablets," and, "The doctors are there to help you if you need it."

Part of the reason why the chest-pumping encouragement wasn't required was because hovering just over our heads, and swooping up and down only 20 metres over the top of us was a helicopter, in which the official photographers and videographers were taking their images. On either side of the start line was a stack of speakers on which was playing Queen, Hotel California and finally, as we all counted down from ten for the start of this life changing event, AC/DC playing 'Highway to Hell'. The excitement and adrenalin was awesome. My heart felt like it was going to explode. People were hopping from foot to foot, punching the air and whooping and hollering as we all cheered and slowly spilt out over the start line. The Marathon des Sables 2010 was underway. OMG I hoped I had done enough training and preparation.

I was in a daze as we all set off. The early pace was very slow as the top runners were in the front and sprinted away, but the vast majority of the rest of us just slowly plodded off. Everyone was pretty much in a group for the first few kilometres, but eventually we started to stretch out. I certainly wasn't near the front, but I wasn't at the back either. As I walked along, with the early morning temperature around 30C, I was going over all of the things I had learnt throughout my training. I was very aware of going out too fast by trying to keep up with those in front, so I purposely slowed myself down. I checked and rechecked my various pockets and pouches, my water bottles and drinking tubes, my hat, my boots and the many other items of gear and caches of food. I knew this was a way of calming myself down, and hey, it worked. I had put three of the electrolyte tablets in each of my water bottles and so far they were working well. The electrolyte tablets became a vital part of my food kit when down at Wilsons Prom. During one of the early 62-kilometre training walks, I had started to wobble all over the track like the lady in the marathon in the 1996 Olympics. The effect then was so bad that I needed to find out what was happening and what to do about it. After some weeks of investigation, I finally learnt that there are high-tech supplements that help overcome this dangerous situation. And these are what I now refer to as the electrolyte tablets.

My food routine, which I will now explain to you, was worked out over the 5000 km of training. I know it sounds oppressively anal, but you must remember that I am type 1 diabetic and food is of vital importance to me every minute of every day. The considerations when choosing the type of food I was bringing with me were the amount of carbohydrate (to stay alive), the number of calories (to stay with in rules of the event), the weight of the food (for both the event rules and my ability to keep going) and the ruggedness of the food (we were in the desert). This means, it needed to withstand the rough handling and the extreme temperatures of 50C plus that I was going to be enduring.

My food cycle spanned a 90-minute period, which was repeated over and over and over during the walking hours. At the start of the 90-minute cycle, I would have a fruit strip. These are individually wrapped strips of fruit pulp that contain 23 grams of carbohydrate. After eating one of these, I would have an almond to clean my teeth and provide a variation of taste and texture. All of this was washed down with a few mouthfuls of water with the electrolytes in it. Twenty minutes later, I repeated this process, then 20 minutes later again. At the 60-minute mark, I replaced the fruit strip with a sports gel, which provided 26 grams of carbohydrate. There was enough carbohydrate in each sports gel to cover a 30-minute period. In addition to the almond, with each gel I would also have a salt tablet, washed down with extra water with electrolytes. Thirty minutes later, the routine started again.

This routine was finely tuned and had been worked out over a long time and many, many kilometres. And joy of joys, it worked. At no point on day one or the next two days did I have a problem with my sugar. This seemingly complex, detailed and anal routine worked brilliantly. If, perchance, I do the event again, I'll be following this same routine.

The Event
Day One

Day One was a total distance of 29km with two checkpoints. The track passed through desert countryside very similar to what I had already experienced in Saudi Arabia, being a changing combination of rough stones, flat, endless mud flats and salt pans, hills of rough rock and some sand. It is one of the misconceptions about deserts that they are made of rolling sand dunes. Of course there are places like that, but the majority of the desert is boring, flat and dry. I learnt at the end of the day that the temperature got as high as 45 C at its peak.

Starting at 8:30 a.m., I finished the stage around 4 p.m. My sugar was fine throughout the whole stage, as was my food, my salt and my water. The gear all worked as planned, thereby justifying the many long, hard hours I had spent training, both around home and down at Wilsons Prom. In fact, the only real difference between the Wilsons Prom walks and what I was encountering now, apart from the lack of greenery obviously, was the heat. But, and this is surprising to myself and everyone I have told, I don't remember giving the heat even a second thought in the Sahara. Maybe this was because I was so utterly focussed on the job at hand.

Everyone soon fell into the routine that they would follow for the rest of the event. For me, this meant just plodding along, one step after the other, at a good, steady pace of approximately 4 kph. People went past me and I later I went past them. For hour after hour, the walking continued. I had my desert hat and wrap-around sunglasses on, so the sun and the glare did not pose a problem.

At around every 12 km, there was a checkpoint. The checkpoints were where they registered the time of your arrival, clipped your water card and gave you a bottle of water, and where you could rest in the shade of a tent or see the medical staff if necessary. Already at CP1, there were a couple of people having their feet attended to, so I didn't like their chances of getting through to the end.

An interesting part of the event was that the end of the allowable time throughout the event was marked by two camels being led along by Berbers, the native people of northern Africa. So long as you stayed in front of these camels, you were travelling within the allowable time. If you fell behind the camels, it meant your time was slower than necessary to finish the stage, and therefore possibly the event, within the allowable time. Luckily for me, I didn't see the camels on day one.

After walking almost non-stop for a bit over seven hours in the blazing sun and temperatures up to 45 C, I finally arrived at the bivouac for that night. It was quite a relief to know that I could now sit down in the shade and rest. The arrival routine, after crossing the finish line and being automatically registered as having finished, was to stagger over to the 'water tent' to get the water card clipped and to collect the four bottle water allotment for the night. The four bottles of precious water were to last all needs and requirements until the next water distribution, which wasn't until 7 o'clock the next morning. One of the little things that I've learnt that I will know in four years is to reserve a bottle of water from this allotment for the start of the stage the next day.

The rest of the day and evening was taken up with reviewing the day with the other tent mates, going over the gear and making repairs and adjustments where necessary, inspecting feet and tape and preparing and eating the evening meal. For me, apart from the ongoing fruit strips and sports gels, I also had meal replacement bars, powdered milk (yum) and a freeze-dried meal. My learning from the previous night was that I didn't need to use the stove to heat water for the freeze dried meal. All I needed to do was to add the water to the meal in the Ziploc bag, seal it, then leave it to sit on the ground in the sun for 10 or 15 minutes. By that time the meal, while not gourmet, was at least edible. There's nothing better than sitting on the stony ground in the middle of the Sahara desert after walking 29km through the heat of the day to change your ideas of what is edible and enjoyable. Cordon bleu it wasn't; nutritious and edible it was.

Not long after the sun disappeared, everyone in the tent settled down for a rough, uncomfortable, uneasy sleep on the rocky ground. Snuggled up in my sleeping bag—bliss.

Day two and the routine started again. Not long after the crack of dawn the teams of Berbers, in a whirlpool of waving arms and cries of, *"Yella, yella!"* hoisted the tent from over us in one unceremonious swoop. It was funny to see as they rapidly moved down the line of tents, everyone still lying on the ground rugs in their sleeping bags but now exposed to the sky.

We all went through our morning routine of food, checking and packing our gear, checking and adjusting foot strapping, lining up to get our morning water allocation and performing our personal ablutions, not necessarily in that order. Being a morning person, I was reasonably comfortable with the process, just working my way through the necessary steps. But someone like Sam, who is a self-confessed and well-established night time person, struggled with the abrupt and early start to the day. One of my important morning activities was to ensure my various pockets contained the right amount of fruit strips and sports gels. I could fit enough in there for about eight hours, so any distance less that 35 km was covered. For anything more than that, I would need to 'recharge' my pockets at one of the checkpoints. Another of my standard activities was to put the electrolyte tablets in my water bottles.

On day one, I was using three electrolyte tablets per bottle, which was the recommended amount. But I had figured out that at that rate, I was going to run out of the tablets before completing the final stage. So I reduced the amount of electrolytes from three to two tablets per bottle, which should give me enough tablets for the final day, and increased the number of salt tablets that I was taking from one per 90 minutes to one each time I ate a fruit strip or sports gel. That was the theory. The reality was yet to present itself.

As this day was the 5th of April and my birthday, the whole group sang happy birthday to me at the start line. It's great hearing a thousand strangers sing you happy birthday with a French accent. Interestingly, there were two other people also celebrating their birthday on that day. I found this interesting simply because, with 1000 people in the event, statistically there should have been three birthdays on each day. And on the 5th of April there were. That's another one of those things that maybe only I find cute.

After the housekeeping announcements, the music and the countdown, we started the stage again to the music of AC/DC blasting out *'Highway to Hell'*. With the temperature set to reach 50C that day, it was an appropriate song. The helicopter swooped over us as we all as we streamed out into the hazy yonder.

We soon found ourselves trekking across a long, flat, boring wasteland with the occasional scrubby bush. Way off in the distance, I could just make out a hazy, almost invisible line of blue hills. As we were heading directly towards these hills, I wondered whether we were going to cross them.

I thought, *No, surely not. They're way too far away and look way too big.*

If I had bothered to look at the road book, which has a map for each day's stage, I would have known if we were. But my approach is 'what will be will be', so I didn't bother with the road book and map. And sure enough, we did.

CP2 was about a kilometre before the base of the line of hills. But before I got there, as I left CP1 and headed out across yet another endless flat plain, my decision to reduce the electrolytes chose to tap me on the shoulder, with the force of a baseball bat, and tell me that it was a bad idea.

Three or four kilometres from CP2, I started to feel my feet and legs losing co-ordination. Soon after, I could sense that I was having trouble walking in a straight line. Then I started to suffer the teeth-clenching cramps in my hamstrings, my groin, my feet and my calves as I struggled to take each step. All of this came over me within a period of only a few minutes. Having felt all of this during my training at Wilsons Prom I knew what it was, but that didn't help get rid of it.

As I staggered along, I started having more salt tablets. But it seemed that no matter how many I had the cramps and staggers wouldn't go away. I stumbled on, taking more and more salt tablets. Instead of one per 20 minutes, I was now having one every ten minutes. And sometimes I would have two together.

But alas! It wasn't enough. While stumbling across an area of rugged and sharp rocks, I staggered like I was amazingly drunk, lost my balance completely with a 14 kg backpack on my back and fell flat on my face, cutting my hand and grazing my arms. I couldn't even lay still and flat on the ground, trying to roll around and flailing with my arms and legs.

This was quite frightening.

From out of nowhere, a 4WD with a couple of doctors in it appeared and they started to bring me around. They got me to sit up, which still wasn't easy, and sit in the shade of the car. They took my temperature and tested my blood sugar, all the while basically ignoring my pleas that I was OK; it was just my salt level. Of course they ignored me because they were the ones with the years of education, so they needed to convince themselves of what was wrong.

They found that my sugar was fine and my temperature was fine, so I must be suffering from not enough salt. In my mind, I thought something like "Duh". Then they started to admonish me for not drinking enough water, not taking my salt tablets and basically not doing the right things. I didn't argue because what was the point? I was drinking all of my water and I was taking many more salt tablets than I was supposed to, so their scalding was misdirected. I knew that so I just smiled, popped a salt tablet in my mouth and said 'thank you'. One of the amazing things about low salt is how quickly you can recover with a rest and a drink of water.

After my brief rest, I was able to get back up and continue, almost as if there had never been a problem. Now I was pushing salt tablets down my neck every five minutes, that is 12 per hour—seriously. This seemed to be enough to keep the problems at bay, for now.

Eventually, I got to CP2, did the usual checkpoint things and then headed off towards the now looming hill. Remember the hazy line of hills I was looking at earlier? Well, here they were and they looked daunting. From a distance of a kilometre or so, I could see a tiny ant line of people making their way up. I sighed and prepared myself for the inevitable slog.

The first part was just a rocky track making its way up, but this became a drift of sand. This was quite difficult, so by the time I got to the top of that, I was huffing and puffing and my legs were complaining. Next came a rocky path up a steep, dry creek gully climbing over rocks. Just as I got to the top of this bit and was about to climb out, I came across two people prostate in the gully with intravenous drips coming out of their arms. It hadn't occurred to me but the conditions were now bad enough that people were dropping. There were medical staff in attendance so I stepped around them and continued up. In a macabre way, those poor people made me feel better. They were suffering big time and I hadn't even realised the conditions were tough.

I joined the ant line of people climbing up the rocks. This was tough and there were heaps of opportunities to fall and break your neck, especially with a heavy backpack on. Meanwhile, the helicopter was swooping and whooshing overhead in an ear-shattering roar.

Finally, at last, I made it to the top. This was a saddle between two peaks with support people there to help as people staggered to the top. My legs were cramping, so I sat down for a rest and again I received the advice to drink more water and have a salt tablet. But by now I knew that I just had to rest for five minutes and I'd be fine.

Once rested, I took off again, now heading down to the bivouac. My time, while not brilliant, was OK, so I just trudged along down a dry creek bed. It was strewn with boulders and was a great place to 'do an ankle', but my experience walking in the same sort of country side in Saudi had taught me to be careful, so all was OK.

The rest of the stage went without fuss and I finally made it to the bivouac.

The rest of the day and the evening followed the routine that had now developed. Water allocation, check and repair gear, check and repair foot tape, talk over the day's highlights with the tent mates, have my evening medication, prepare and eat food, prepare sleeping area for the night, a little socialising with neighbouring tents, settle down for the night and suffer the hard ground. Easy really. One addition for the food tonight was mashed potato. Even though I didn't add quite enough water and the mashed potato was a bit chewier than it should have been, as a supplement for the freeze-dried food, the mashed potato was a success.

The day ended under a brilliant dome of stars. You haven't lived until you have seen a night sky in the desert.

The Event
Day Three

Day three and the whole routine started again. The main difference today was that people were starting to show the punishment they have suffered over the previous days and were becoming a little more subdued. Today's stage was 39 km long, a distance which during training would have taken me eight hours. But judging by my experience from the first two days, I expected it would take me around nine and a half hours.

The start was a little different in that we had to gather at the start line 15 minutes earlier than normal so they could take the '25' photo. This was where all of the competitors stood within a '25' stencil made of ropes and the helicopter took many photographs.

Once we started, everything progressed as normal. I was now very good at pacing myself, having learnt to resist the temptation to rush to keep up with the quicker competitors. The track was straight and flat, crossing country that was stony and with thin scrubby bushes every now and occasionally. The walking progressed as normal except that, after not long at all, I started to wobble again. Today it happened surreptitiously, sneaking up on me without me even noticing.

I suddenly found myself staggering again, so I started eating salt tablets and drinking more water. But this didn't help enough and before I realised what had happened, I staggered and fell over again, flat on my face. Because this was only 4 km from the start there were still people close by, so I heard a couple of the emergency whistles going off and people shouting for assistance. I momentarily wondered who they were concerned about, but then realised it was me.

As I rolled over onto my back, a camera was pushed in front of me as one of the news crews tried to capture the moment. Then I heard angry voices as those around me tried to get the attention of a doctor instead of a fellow with a camera. There was no doctor around and I had assured the people who were trying to help that I was OK. I ate a couple more salt tablets, had a guzzle of water and a short rest, then got to my feet and kept going. Due to the fuss with the salt on day two, I had decided to risk running out of the electrolyte tablets by having two and a half per bottle of water instead of two. But obviously this was not enough on its own to keep my electrolytes up, so I needed to continue to have a lot of salt tablets. I got going again and, with the extra salt tablets each hour, all was OK. I reached CP1 OK and went through the normal routine.

The ground was very rocky after leaving CP1. I was walking on my own when yet again, I found the salt was suddenly low. A quick couple of salt tablets and a dose of denial surprisingly didn't fix it and again I found myself on my face. This time there were doctors within sight, so they were quickly on the scene. They sat me in the shade of a tree and started doing tests. They checked my sugar and found that it was slightly low, so out came the satchel of sugar again. I knew now that they did this with everyone, not just me. The sugar test was given to everyone who went face down. They took my temperature and then announced the funniest thing I'd heard all day; my temperature was up, so I must have been suffering a fever. I chuckled and asked them if they had noted where we were. As English was a distant second language for them they didn't understand the humour, so I just let it ride. However, I was concerned that they might try to make me withdraw or want to give me a saline drip or something. Fortunately, this wasn't the case. They really just wanted me to rest, to show them that I was drinking my water and taking my salt tablets. Once I had rested, watered and salted myself they let me continue on.

The day progressed with one step following the other, over and over and over. We found ourselves walking across a salt flat that appeared to have no end. It was utterly flat and the track was utterly straight. We just kept walking on and on and on without end.

Step,

Step,

Step,

Plod,

Plod,

Plod… without end.

I was to find out later that just as I was coming to CP2, after walking a dead straight line across the salt flat for 12 kilometres, the temperature was 56 C. I didn't know that and didn't even realise it was particularly hot. I just kept walking. Apart from putting one foot in front of the other, the only other thing I knew was that there was somebody walking not far behind me all across the salt flat. I considered stopping and letting them go past, but I didn't have the energy to change my pace. So I just kept plodding on, step, step, step, hoping eventually to get to the checkpoint.

I was to learn later that the person walking behind me was a fellow Australian who decided that the pace I was walking was a good pace for him, so he slotted in behind me and let me do the pace keeping. It is a technique for saving brain power. You get in behind someone and just stay there, without the need to make decisions or think about much at all. When the conditions are as harsh as we had over that salt flat, it's a good way to conserving vital energy.

We made it to CP2 as if in a dream.

After the normal checkpoint checks and balances, as well as a rest of 15 minutes I set off again, this time bound for CP3. A British lady, Sarah Jane, was setting off at the same time, so we decided to walk together. Sarah-Jane appeared to be suffering more than I was, as she had the side effects of the bug that had been sweeping through the camp. She had a badly upset stomach and felt like, well let's just say she felt really bad. Twice we had to stop while she went off the track, and I turned my back, for her to relieve herself. I began to wonder how she could possibly even get to the next checkpoint. She had little energy, a bad stomach and a slight fever.

We kept walking at a slightly slower pace than I would have done if I was on my own, so I kept reassuring her that I was benefitting from walking with her as it was slowing me down when I probably needed it. And this was the truth, even though she thought I was just being kind. We plodded on and on and I was amazed at how she was able to just keep going.

Finally, we made it to a tree with some shade where there were two other people enjoying the rest. This was a young British couple who were boyfriend and girlfriend. He was suffering the same ailment that Sarah-Jane was suffering, but they had already had a decent rest under the tree. When some doctors came along in their 4WD, they first attended to the young couple, giving him advice and a satchel of magic powder. Then they turned their attention to Sarah-Jane. I was sure she was going to call it quits as she had been considering that option as we walked along. Because she was now in the care of the doctors, I left with the young couple and we continued on.

For the next hour, we plodded along, with the young fellow suffering terribly from the effects of the bug. His girlfriend was beside herself with concern but was quite fit and healthy herself. She was trying to convince the fellow to call it quits the next time they saw a doctor, but he kept resisting. Eventually, along came a 4WD with some doctors and her attempts to convince him stepped up a notch.

Did I mention that the temperature was 56 C?

As they were now in the care of doctors, I kept going. Step after step I was heading for CP3. I was not doing too well myself, feeling the salt constantly tapping me on the shoulder. On and on and on, step after step after step, the country was flat and endless. I was thinking about the electrolyte tablets and the obvious fact that I needed at least three per bottle of water. I calculated this with the distance left in the event and the number of bottles of water. It didn't compute. No matter how I tweaked it I was going to run out of the electrolyte tablets before I finished the final stage. I had miscalculated the required number by one tube of 20 tablets. DAMN! I had brought four tubes with me when I should have brought five. DAMN! I wondered whether I could effectively substitute the lack of electrolyte tablets with salt tablets, but the previous day's experiences, combined with my experiences so far today told me that it wasn't possible. The electrolyte tablets gave me something necessary that the salt tablets just didn't have.

DAMN!

I don't know how long I continued to plod along by myself across the seemingly endless plain, but it can't have been too long; it just seemed like it. In the distance, I could see the start of small sand dunes, so at least the endless flat had some respite. Now I was thinking of the next day, which was the 80 km day that was going to take me at least 24 hours and more likely 30 hours. I had already had two bouts of low salt today, episodes that are quite frightening to endure, and I had determined that I didn't have enough electrolyte tablets to finish the event. Now, as I plodded towards the sand dunes, I simply ran out of energy. For the first time in the event, I stopped and stood there, contemplating my future. I didn't stand for long, convincing myself after 30 seconds to take a step and continue walking, but now I felt like an empty bag of skin. There were no muscles or bones left, just skin. I could have curled up on the ground right there and gone to sleep amongst the scorpions.

Right at that very inopportune moment, a 4WD with a couple of doctors drove up to me. They made the usual thumbs up sign through their closed, air-conditioned window and I looked at them. They made the sign again and my decision was made. I made the sign of a knife across my throat and the Marathon des Sables 2010 was over for me. That was my moment of decision and once made, I couldn't go back on it.

I had spent two years of my life training myself to be the driver of my own destiny, to take full and utter responsibility for my safety and my life, so when my decision was made to call it quits I couldn't go back on that decision. If I did, it meant that every decision I ever made again in my life was negotiable, and I can't live with my diabetes with that sort of soft 'n fuzzy control. After hours of thinking, considering, 'what-if-ing', manipulating, trying to find any way that I could get my salt through to the finish line, I had now made my decision to withdraw.

And oh, how I have pondered that decision since!

The doctors spent 30 minutes trying to convince me to change my mind, but I held tight to my decision. I knew that I had made it for the right reasons and to change my mind and continue would have been seriously risking my life. I sat in the shade of their 4WD and drank some water. They were talking on their radio in French and stopping every now and then to see if I was ready to continue. I kept telling them that I was out but they struggled to understand my commitment. Eventually they came to realise that I wasn't going to change my mind, so the withdrawal process began.

They loaded my gear and myself into the 4WD and we started bouncing across the desert in the general direction of the checkpoint. Even while driving back they were constantly on the lookout for other competitors who might be in difficulty. I saw that, judging by my experience of driving in the desert in Saudi Arabia, these guys were excellent off-roaders. Having a diesel powered Toyota certainly helped.

Back at the checkpoint, the processing of my withdrawal continued. They asked me a few questions and filled in a form. Then I sat there for a painful hour, watching other competitors come in to the checkpoint, get their water, have a rest then continue on towards the end of the stage. I saw the young British couple come in which really surprised me. The girl had finally continued walking on her own and had arrived under her own steam. Then while I was there her boyfriend, who had convinced the doctors that he was OK, also came in. So after the euphoric reunion, they set off again, sharing painful bliss. I really thought he was out, but he had kept on going. This event was an amazing show of human endurance.

We finally made it back to the bivouac by late afternoon and, after being fully processed and having my race number taken away, I went to the tent, where all of my tent mates were already into their evening routine. When a person withdraws, they are supposed to hand over all their food to the officials, so there is no chance that they will give some of their food to other competitors. When they asked me to hand over my food, I told them I couldn't because I was diabetic. I thought that this could lead to a serious problem if they insisted, but fortunately they saw common sense and allowed me to keep it, with the promise from me that I wouldn't give any away. They trusted me to keep my word, so I honoured their trust and didn't give any away. I believe this may have led to a small amount of resentment with one or two of my tent mates, but I hope I'm wrong with that. Food is the most important thing in the world to a type 1 diabetic and having a reliable supply is essential. This may be difficult for a healthy person to comprehend.

During the evening a number of people came up to me to offer their commiserations. One was Jay, the organiser for the competitors from North America, Australia and New Zealand. Jay doesn't say much, but with seven MdS's under his belt, he does understand the trauma and heartache associated with pulling out. He offered me kind words and was the first to say what I came to hear a number of times; my decision was the correct one given the circumstances and that I was brave to take that decision. I appreciated his words but it was too early for me to feel happy about it. The other tent mates seemed a little uncomfortable, probably because they didn't know what to say. Meghan did say that she was sorry I had pulled out, which was nice of her.

For the rest of that night, we went through the standard routines. But for me, there was the heavy cloud of withdrawal and no longer being an active participant overhanging everything.

I was not happy.

The Real World Beckons

The next four days, which was the remainder of the event, pretty much ran into each other from my perspective. Virtually from the moment I withdrew from the race at the end of day three, I no longer felt like I was part of it all. No doubt it was only in my head, but I now felt outside what was going on.

The daily routine for those who withdrew but chose to stay with the event began with breakfast in the official food tent, sitting with some of the volunteer workers. More people joined the group of withdrawees each day, so by Day Seven, there were around 50 of us bouncing across the desert in the old Mercedes mini buses.

As I expected, the breakfast that was provided did not fulfil my food requirements, so I was constantly topping up from my race food. No matter where I went or what I was doing, for the rest of my time away from home I had a small selection of race food in my pocket. Even though I was no longer walking across the Sahara desert, I was still a long way from civilisation and a regular food supply, so in essence, I still had to be self-sufficient. Thank goodness the race officials relented and let me keep my food.

Immediately after breakfast was finished, they loaded us into the mini buses, ready to bounce and crash to the next bivouac. Now let me explain these mini buses to you. Once upon a time, these Mercedes mini buses would have been wonderful. But that was once upon a time. Now, after many years of rough Moroccan driving, they were beyond their prime. For a start, none of the bench seats were bolted to the floor, so every time there was a serious bash across a ditch or rock, the bench seats would move. Next, they let every bit of dust that the desert owned inside, so there were times when the inside was a cloud of choking dust. It seemed that whatever suspension they once boasted was now just a dim memory. The radio/cassette player was welded onto a local station, so for four days we enjoyed the Moroccan top of the pops. I have nothing against Arabic music, but hearing what sounded like the same piece of music for four days tended to get toward the repetitive.

Loading us into the buses didn't mean that we were going anywhere. We often sat there for nearly an hour as the drivers and their organisers decided where we were going, how we were going to get there, what time we needed to arrive and whatever other detail needed deciding before we could leave. It was funny sitting there watching, as I like to do, as people in the bus got restless and would choose to leave the bus to stretch their legs. You could almost guarantee that no sooner had a couple of people left than the drivers would decide it was time to leave. Then the search would begin for the people who were missing. They would eventually come back but now the drivers had been side-tracked. On the final day, we had Spanish, Italians, French, Americans, New Zealanders a

Paraguayan and me on the bus, so keeping this mixture of people together was only slightly easier than herding cats.

Our driver was great. I stayed in the same bus and had the same driver for the whole four days. I was told his name but can't remember, so I'll call him Abdul. He was a native Berban and appeared to be running a side business as local 'fixer' while also driving us around. We ended up calling him Schumaker, as his driving skills in the rough of the desert were beyond question. No matter where we were in this vast wilderness, Abdul knew somebody and was regularly waving at someone and yelling out a greeting. His mobile phone was often stuck to his head as he shouted instructions down the line. We were regularly stopping at some wayward, haphazard-looking building where Abdul would jump from the driver's seat while the bus was still moving and run over to see a fellow inside. A minute or two later, he would reappear, jump back in the driver's seat and off we'd go again.

Abdul didn't like to play follow the leader, so when we were meant to be part of an orderly convoy making its way towards a set destination, Abdul would get frustrated with the slow pace and set off along a shortcut. More than once his mobile phone would ring, there'd be a brief but loud exchange of information, then Abdul would hang back and we'd join the convoy again.

The most important thing for us to do while enjoying our desert crossing was to hang on. The jumping and lurching and rocking and rolling would have taken a much harsher toll on us if we weren't all gripping on for grim life. That, combined with the un-tethered seats, meant that our bumpy journey across the desert was an endurance event in itself.

On the longer journeys, we'd stop at one of the rare trees and sit in the shade to eat our bagged lunch. My fellow travellers soon came to learn that I had special food requirements, so would pass over their peanuts and cheeses while I handed out the various items that I couldn't eat. It was a good arrangement that led to them asking me questions about my MdS experiences and the diabetes.

On one of the journeys, somewhere in the middle of the Moroccan Sahara, we came across a house and family seemingly in the middle of nowhere. Abdul stopped the bus and we all clambered out for a stretch. There was a well there, with the rope and bucket, and someone raised a bucket of water. I looked at the water, which I certainly wouldn't volunteer to drink, then the young children and where we were, i.e., the middle of nowhere, and then considered where I lived and the environment of my existence. I won't get philosophical here, but seeing the extreme conditions some people still live in really does give you a moment to pause and ponder.

A couple of interesting things happened during this time. Because I was wearing the satellite tracking device, Donna and any number of other people were watching when I stopped. Unfortunately, due to where we were and the extreme conditions we were in, it was a full 36 hours before I was finally able to make an expensive satellite telephone call and tell Donna what had happened and that I was alright.

On the evening of the second last day, it is a tradition that the organisers of the event bring a French orchestra in by helicopter. So all afternoon the helicopters were flying back and forth as they brought in a whole orchestra and their instruments for what ended up being a spell-binding evening of entertainment in the desert.

It was while sitting there watching the orchestra under the desert stars that I realised that I wasn't clearly seeing what was happening on stage. I had double vision and no matter how much I blinked and wiped my eyes, it just wasn't going away. I was sitting with Meghan at the time and she may have wondered why I was being quiet, but I was rather concerned that I couldn't see what was going on very well. Finally I figured it out, I was having only the second hypoglycaemia episode since getting to the desert seven days previously. That was something to be happy about, but right now I had to catch my hypo before it took over and rendered me incapable of helping myself. I guesstimate that I was less than 15 minutes from oblivion when it finally turned the corner from all of the food I ate as quickly as I could. Being a type 1 diabetic can have detrimental consequences in so many ways, with Meghan now possibly considering that I'm a little strange.

The remainder of the event, four days for me, passed this way for everyone who withdrew but chose to stay with the event. Even though it was heart-wrenching after all of the hard work and commitment, it did provide an opportunity to see the human spirit in action. Some examples that I became aware of are:

- Sarah-Jane, after suffering from the bug all day on day three, finished the event
- Madhu, whose feet were like plates of minced meat at the end of day two, finished the event
- The young boyfriend/girlfriend British couple that I was walking with, finished the event

- A number of blind runners, being guided by a friend and a tether, finished the event. This one choked me up when I first saw a blind runner cross the line at the end of the 82 km stage
- Older people who looked as if they were close to death, continuing on and finishing the event

That is the most extraordinary part of the Marathon des Sables that the rest of the world struggles to comprehend. It is a living example of how the Human Spirit (notice the capitals) can soar and beat almost any adversity. I'll be back in four years!

The 25th running of the Marathon des Sables was now over, but my adventure wasn't. We were now at the finish line and the early runners were starting to come in. The first to cross was the local hero Mohammed, who finished in an extraordinary time considering what he had been through over the previous six days. The TV cameras were all over him when he crossed and he was interviewed like a Hollywood celebrity.

The fast runners crossed the finish line over the next ten minutes, all having completed the final 25 km in a fairly close bunch. I stayed there until the fastest Australian, Stuart from Melbourne, finished then, after congratulating him, walked around to see who else had finished. People were crossing the line in regular clumps now, but my feeling of exclusion persisted. There was no denying that I had not experienced the hardships of the last four days that the people now coming across the line had, so I could not fully share their experiences.

So I found my allocated coach for the trip back to Ouarzazate and boarded for the six-hour ride.

The journey back was picturesque, long and uneventful. As I was no longer nervous with anticipation as I was on the journey there nine days ago, I was able to see more clearly the countryside, towns and villages that we were driving through. Morocco is a very interesting and beautiful place, a mixture of typical Middle Eastern third world and the modern world. Out in country Morocco, there are some very picturesque towns; many of the villages are like they would have been 50 years ago, with donkeys a common form of transport and women walking down the road fully covered with their black veils. There were children riding bicycles and playing ball games as our convoy of coaches drove through.

After many hours, we finally rounded a bend in the highway and saw the lake which meant we were close to Ouarzazate. Not long after we were at the hotel and collecting our bags.

The rest of that afternoon and evening were probably the loneliest I experienced during my entire journey. Everyone who completed the event, which meant the majority of the people there, were still on a euphoric high from having completed such a gruelling exercise. There was lots of excitement as people found their rooms, quickly showered and changed their clothes for the first time in over a week, then started gathering in groups to again go over what they had accomplished. It was important that I contact Donna by email, as it had now been three days since the single satellite telephone conversion in which I had told her that I was still alive, so I found the email connection and battled with the French keyboard.

Unfortunately, I misjudged the timing for my evening injection. I should have clarified what time the dinner room was going to open before having my jab because by the time the food was available, I was sinking rapidly into a serious hypo. This is where my Manhattan friend whom I mentioned earlier in the story became a real friend. He came and sat at my table as we waited for the food to be ready and asked me if everything was OK. I had enough brain power left to be honest and tell him that no, everything wasn't alright; my sugar was dropping quickly. He immediately took charge and hassled the waiters until they got me an orange juice, then stayed on their case until they got me another one. Looking back at that moment, I can now see that I was on the edge of a dramatically bad situation, but was saved from further drama by my New York friend. If you are reading this in Manhattan, thank you very much.

This situation is a classic example of how type 1 diabetes never lets you forget and relax. For the sake of ten or 15 minutes which, to a healthy person, may be reason to whinge that the food is taking too long, a type 1 diabetic can be left incapable and potentially in hospital.

The dinner was finally ready and was very nice. We ate our fill and then wandered off, looking for entertainment. Everybody by now was separating off into groups to celebrate through the evening. I looked for my tent mates but found they were spread from one side of the hotel to the other. Eventually, I decided that an early night in bed was probably called for, so called the day over. A sad result of this is that I didn't get to say goodbye properly to anyone. What a shame!

The next morning, I rose very early in order to get the email computer before it was taken over by the hordes.

Getting access to emails in the middle of Morocco is not easy and, as there were a lot of people following my progress, I needed to let them know how things were going. This morning, I was much more careful about having my injection and the timing of the food. But I had learnt from the previous evening that it wasn't just the timing of the food that was a possible concern, but also the nature of the food. So I found myself yet again being self-sufficient with my food, almost as if I was back in the Sahara desert. I filled my pocket with the fruit strips and sports gels just in case the food in the dining room was late, as well as delayed my injection for as long as was sensible. Sure enough, I needed to dip into my special food before the breakfast was ready.

As breakfast was spread over about two hours, and I'm notoriously an early bird, I didn't get to see any of my tent mates in the morning, either over breakfast or after. They must have all been enjoying the pleasure of a sleep-in after the rough sleeps and early risings during the event. So after having breakfast, doing emails, packing my bags and walking around looking for my tent mates without any success, I sadly left the hotel at 11 o'clock to walk the 15 minutes to the hotel I stayed at when we first arrived in Ouarzazate, where I was to meet my friend Nick from England.

To Marrakesh and Beyond

And there he was. After ten years, my friend Nick was sitting by the pool waiting for my arrival. After all these years, here we were meeting again in a faraway corner of Morocco. It was great to see him.

Nick hadn't changed much since I last saw him as we said goodbye to each other at Riyadh airport in April 2000. His forehead was a little more pronounced and his belt was a little bigger, but apart from that, he was the same Nick. After our greetings, we sat on the poolside lounges for half an hour and swapped stories before going up to the room and settling in. Nick was here to help ensure that my sugar was OK as I recovered from the event. This had all been organised months ago when it was expected that I would be completing the full distance. But because I had actually pulled out four days previously, it wasn't so important for Nick to look after me so we could just enjoy being in Morocco and reminiscing about old times. There were lots of memories and 'Remember whens' because the time Nick shared with myself, Donna and the girls in Saudi Arabia was a very important time for all of us.

After settling in to the room, we went for the obligatory walk to the supermarket. This time I knew where it was from the first visit, so we went straight there and filled some bags with groceries. We bought way too much because it's much safer to have too much than to not have enough. The groceries we bought here needed to last me for the rest of the day and evening, breakfast the next day then the trip back to Marrakesh. And if you think back, I hadn't been able to do a supermarket trip the previous afternoon and had a rather bad hypo in the evening. The hypo was not *because* I didn't go to a supermarket, but if I had been able to visit a supermarket, I wouldn't have had the hypo. See the connection? Yes? Now you are starting to see the world through the eyes of a type 1 diabetic. Some people call it 'anal'; I call it 'survival'.

That night, Nick and I walked up the road to the same restaurant that Erick, Sam and I went to before the event. There we had the same lovely meal that included a tagine. I wish I could tell you more about this little restaurant, because it is lovely. The setting is beautiful, the food wonderful and the service excellent. We will certainly be returning when I do the event again in four years—yes, the decision has been made. 2014 is when I complete the Marathon des Sables.

The restaurant tonight was full of people. Last time there were many empty tables, but this night it was so full that we only just managed to get a seat. Sitting at another table were a group of MdS competitors including Denis, a very friendly Irishman who owns a restaurant in country France. He was one of the memorable characters.

* * * * * * *

Monday the 12th of April and the goal today was to travel from Ouarzazate back to Marrakesh, where we had a villa booked in the Medina for five nights. We had asked the hotel the previous afternoon to arrange for a taxi for us, similar to my trip with Erick and Sam from Marrakesh. This time the taxi fare was 1200 dirhams, which converts to around $A185. Yes, you could say that was a bit much, but the comfort and the convenience of being able to stop anywhere we wanted to was worth it. Our driver was great, being a local fellow with a family from a village not far out of Ouarzazate. He proudly showed us where his village was as we drove past towards the Atlas Mountains.

Speaking of the Atlas Mountains, as I was now taking much more notice of my surroundings compared to the first trip, they are extraordinarily beautiful. They are a long line of snow topped mountains that run through the heart of Morocco from south west to north east. The road between Ouarzazate to Marrakesh runs directly across the mountains, taking in spectacular scenery and some interesting country towns and villages.

We stopped twice along the way, once at a large traveller's café for a cup of tea and again at the main town in the mountains. A strange thing happened when we stopped at the town for a stretch and to answer the call of nature. I came to realise that this was one of the very few spots I recognised along the whole trip from my original trip nine days previously with Erick and Sam. I mentioned this to Nick, momentarily a little concerned that I might be losing my mind. But we concluded that I must have been so very focussed and more than a little stressed about the upcoming event on the first trip, so that not much made its way into my over-stressed brain. Now I was actually seeing the countryside and it was beautiful.

After five hours of a very pleasant drive, we arrived in Marrakesh. The driver found our villa by calling the fellow who managed the villa, Abdulleila, on his mobile and getting directions. I found even this amazing because as far as I could see, the Medina (the old part of the city) was simply a rabbit warren of laneways and impossible to navigate. So how anyone could understand instructions over a mobile phone left me stumped.

Our abode for the next five nights was an amazing looking place that I can highly recommend. It is called Villa Dar Musique. It is buried deep in a labyrinth of alleyways that will feature a little more later in the story. The lovely people who run the villa, Abdulleila and 'the sisters', are wonderful, with Abdulleila more than happy to provide advice, directions and anything else to make your stay in the Medina as fulfilling as possible.

The original plan was for between eight and ten of us to be staying at the villa, but the problem with Donna's back, plus other things that came up as time passed, meant that it was only Nick and I there for the whole five days.

* * * * * * *

Our first breakfast time back in Marrakesh was interesting from the start. As we didn't have an opportunity the previous day to go to a supermarket, I was rather reliant on the breakfast provided at the villa. And as we were now working on 'Inshallah time', that is the more relaxed idea of time that prevails in the Middle East, exactly when breakfast was going to be ready was anyone's guess. And as we were effectively stuck in the labyrinth of laneways that make up the Medina until we had a chance to explore and work it all out, getting backup food was not possible. So I needed to revert to my race food that I still had left over to get me through until breakfast was finally served. So once again, three days after the event finished and seven days since I had withdrawn from the event, I was again needing to be self-sufficient. This made me wonder what would have happened had I been successful and finished the event. We would still be here at the villa, but I would have eaten my way through all of my race food earlier. What would I have had to get me through?

Breakfast did come, close to 9:30 as it so happens, and it was beautiful. Freshly squeezed orange juice, a Moroccan dish made from eggs and tomatoes and some lightly spiced rice, not exactly what we expect in the west, but we weren't in the west. We were in the Medina in Marrakesh in Morocco.

We used that day to firstly, and definitely most importantly, find a supermarket. Abdulleila gave directions we could follow that took us to the outside of the Medina, down a crowded road full of cars, motor bikes, the occasional donkey, street markets and the general throng and humdrum of Marrakesh. Just walking the couple of kilometres to the supermarket was fascinating in itself. The smells, the sounds, the things we saw were all just amazing. For me, Marrakesh was a mixture of Riyadh in Saudi Arabia and Bangalore in India, with a touch of Venice thrown in for good measure. It was a wonderful walk of discovery.

The supermarket was a full-on, genuine supermarket of a size and type that we would expect in Australia. It had everything we could expect on the shelves, including a brand of gluten free breakfast food. For not the first time this trip I breathed a sigh of relief and thought 'thank heavens'. Apart from the breakfast food, we bought bottles of water, some fresh fruit, UHT milk (always a good thing to have in warm climates with no access to refrigeration) and a bunch of comfort food. All of this made both of us feel more comfortable and relaxed, knowing that we had ready access to good food. For Nick, this was just a relaxing feeling. For me, it was a feeling of safety. One interesting thing I found is that the only brand names that we recognised were Coca Cola and Green Giant. Everything else on the shelves, without exception, were either local brands or French. That's another one of those things that you probably don't find interesting, but I do.

I know, I know; you're not the first person to say that.

After the interesting walk back to the villa and having a cup of tea, it was time for our first explore of the Medina. The main, central focus of the old city of Marrakesh is the Jamaa El Fna, which is a big, open square which seems to be constantly on the go. This is where the snake charmers play their music during the day to entice the cobras to dance, where at night there are storytellers and buskers, dancers and restaurants seemingly by the hundred. It is a whirlpool of activity morning, noon and night.

Surrounding the square are many shops selling local wares as well as restaurants where you can enjoy the many tagine meals on offer. The tagine is a particularly Moroccan dish, cooked in a conical terracotta pot that seems to enhance the flavours of the lamb or chicken or beef and the vegetables. They are wonderful, good value and a great meal. Nick and I ended up eating a lot of tagines while enjoying the always interesting vista of El Fna square.

I found an internet café down one of the small roads that lead off El Fna, so took the opportunity to catch up on emails and let Donna and the girls know that I was still alive. This was an interesting experience. Firstly, and before I could even find out about the secondly, again this was a French keyboard and was therefore difficult to use. For example, where on Earth was the @ symbol? On a western keyboard, at least every one that I've ever used, the @ is on top of the '2' key. If you're reading this online now, have a look. I bet it's there. Well, on a French keyboard, chances are it's not. I experienced two versions of French keyboards while in Morocco; one was missing the @ altogether and the other would have it on a different key. With the second, it was a case of finding it and remembering where it was. With the first, the only way I could figure out how to get an @ was to get an email address and copy the @ from that address and then paste it where I needed it. Sounds complicated? Uh huh, it is. A similar situation existed for the _ and the _, but that's another story.

So, after finding the various keys and symbols, I ran head long into the 'secondly', the slowest internet connection I have experienced in years. It was painfully slow, so every email became a mission. But it was cheap, easy to get to and open until 10 o'clock at night.

After a very pleasant afternoon of exploring, it was time to make our way back to the villa. This was my opportunity to learn how to get there. I must take my hat off to Nick here and say that, having done this little walk only twice previously during the one night he was at the villa before coming to Ouarzazate, he had a great memory of which way to go. I couldn't and didn't remember it that well. More on that later.

For now, we left El Fna down a side street, walked through what we came to know as 'Donkey Square', down that alleyway over there, past these shops and the butcher with the meat hanging on hooks, past the bookshop that I was to discover isn't always there, past the pictures hanging on the wall, past the line of jewellery shops to the T intersection facing the Café Bougainvillea. Turned left there and walked for around 150 meters then turned right under the archway, opposite the little shop that looked like it might be a pharmacy of some sort. Now we walked down the laneway and turned left, then turned right towards the white door with the pattern on it, but before getting there turned left again and walked through the tunnel, but watching out for motorbikes coming the other way. We didn't need to worry about it being dark inside because everyone seems to bchave themselves in Morocco. Turned right halfway through the tunnel, then headed towards the daylight, which is about 20 m away. After leaving the tunnel, turned left at the funny symbol scrawled on the wall, then walked down the alleyway for, ummmm, around 50 m. Now, we needed to remember which door was the one to the villa, because they all looked very similar. When we believed we had identified the correct door, we knocked and waited for Abdulleila to open up. And miracle of miracles, there we were.

Now, if you have made notes of the above description I must warn you that the description is valid only for daylight hours and when the shops are open. When the shops close they pull down roller doors and shutters, so effectively they disappear. Plus the open air displays, such as the paintings, simply vanish. So now you have lost half of your landmarks within minutes. At night time, the lights come on, so what was dark is now brightly lit, and what was exposed to daylight may now be lost in the dark. Finding your way back to the villa at night becomes a whole new adventure.

* * * * * * * *

It was now Wednesday the 14th of April and the main goal for the day was to walk around the outside wall of the Medina, a distance of approximately 12 km according to the simple map we had. The reasons for doing this included seeing more of Marrakesh, plus to see part of Marrakesh outside the Medina. The old part of the city was quite different to the rest of Marrakesh and Nick and I wanted to see something of the rest of the city.

We set off at about 10 o'clock, using the main post office in El Fna square as the reference point. We were both wearing backpacks with food and water, so were prepared for a longish walk.

The walking was interesting, with lots of traffic, donkeys and motor bikes. There was nothing of riveting interest beyond the general mayhem that constituted street life in Marrakesh. We walked along leisurely for about four hours, stopping off along the way at a café for a coffee and a good look at the passing street life. This was the real life in Marrakesh, as there were no tourists and not even any French people. Of course Nick and I attracted a bit of interest because we were possibly the only non-Moroccans in the area.

After four hours and the worry that we were lost at a couple of points, we suddenly found ourselves back at our starting point. We had walked around the Medina on the outside of the wall and had seen a good portion of the real Marrakesh.

As we entered back into the Medina through El Fna square, we stopped at a street café for lunch. I had a simple salad and Nick had a tuna salad. Buying anything like this was always a lottery because the menus were written in two languages; Arabic and French. Our Arabic was poor and our French wasn't much better, although Nick did a reasonable job of working out what the French was trying to tell us.

At last, after a wearying day of walking through the throng of the city, we made our way back to the villa. Our intention was to make our way up to the rooftop garden, sit on the lounges with a bottle of Sauvignon Blanc and some nibblies and while the rest of the afternoon away. That was our intention.

The reality was a little different. After we had settled down and got comfortable, Nick started acting a little odd, so I kept my eye on him. His talking slowed down and became sporadic and then, when he tried to go over to a lounge to lie down, he started to stagger noticeably. He staggered back to his chair and sat back down, now as white as a ghost. I was getting concerned.

I went over to check the door to the staircase down from the roof to see if it was locked, so I'd know if Nick and I could go down that way if necessary. The staircase we had used to come up did not have a handrail and I was starting to think that I may have to carry Nick down. When I turned around to tell him that the door was locked, Nick was looking very strange. He wasn't responding to my questions. I went over to him and saw that he was whiter than a ghost, his eyes were wide, staring and unseeing and his arms were stuck straight out in front of him. He wasn't responding to my voice at all and I realised that he was having a mild seizure. I talked calmly to him for about a minute, trying to calm him down. Finally he slowly lowered his arms and his eyes came back into focus. He got some colour back into his face and he began to respond to my voice. His seizure was passing.

When he was able to hold a conversation and could stand without falling, we slowly and carefully went back downstairs. There he went to his bed to lie down for a while. After confirming that his problem was passed and that he was going to be OK, I took the key and walked up to the internet café to do some emails.

That night Nick was fine. As we sat in one of the restaurants having a lovely tagine for dinner, looking out over the amazing night time entertainment in the square, we laughed and joked about what had happened. The theories of the cause extended from walking too far in the warm weather to something not quite right with the tuna salad. The second one had the greater ring of truth to it, so we settled on that.

After dinner, Nick headed back to the villa and I headed off to the internet café. He was fine by now, so there wasn't any risk in letting him walk back by himself. I spent an hour or so doing emails on the world's slowest internet connection and with the oldest computers known to mankind, then headed back towards the villa. Now, if you were to go back up to where I describe how to find the villa, you'll notice that I say that at night time it all looks different. Add to that a case of unrecognised low sugar and what we now have is 'an interesting situation'.

I managed to find the right hand turn under the archway, but after that, it all came off the rails. In the myriad of laneways left and right, in my confused state, it was impossible for me to find the villa. For about 30 minutes, I wandered left and right. Not only couldn't I find it but, as time went on, it was getting even less likely that I would eventually find it.

When I realised that I couldn't even find my way out of the maze back to the road, I finally accepted that my sugar was low and I was lost. But here's a frightening aspect of low sugar; you get to a state where you forget to, or don't want to, or refuse to, eat. So now I was lost, low in sugar, confused and getting worse and yet doing nothing to help fix the situation.

Just then I walked passed a couple of young guys, whom I think I had walked passed a couple of times previously. This time they asked me if everything was alright. I paused for a moment and thought about what to say. My natural response was to say that everything was OK, but as I was lost and it was getting worse, I relented and said, "No, I'm lost."

"Oh," they said. "Whereabouts? Are you staying?" Surprisingly, I could remember the name of the villa, so told them. They said they knew where it was and could show me. I thanked them and then followed as they walked around a couple of corners and stopped at a door. I didn't recognise the door and questioned if this was it. The leader of the two sighed and rolled his eyes almost imperceptibly and assured me it was the correct door, so I knocked. Sure enough Nick opened the door. I breathed a sigh of relief and said thank you to the young fellows.

They then said, "We helped you find your home," to which I said, "Yes, you did. Thank you." Now keep in mind that my sugar was low, so I hadn't clicked to where this was going. They then said, "Now you should give us a present." I thought this was a strange thing to say, then suddenly understood that they were asking for money. I was sad at this, but hey, they did help me home when I really needed it. I got out my wallet and gave them 50 dirhams and said, "Thank you." They were now happy and went on their way.

Back inside, Nick was expressing his concern about me being so late. I explained that my sugar was low and proceeded to eat considerable amounts of emergency food for the next 20 minutes until my sugar started coming back up.

With Nick's problem, me getting lost and then having a hypo, this day had been an interesting one.

* * * * * * * *

Thursday the 15th and things were about to start getting interesting. The day started off as normal, with me having my 'proper' breakfast at a normal time and then having the 'official' breakfast at about 9:30. As we prepared ourselves for the day's activities, the TV was on the BBC and we started hearing reports of a volcano in Iceland. This was just another story amongst the many other stories, so we hardly gave it a second thought.

We decided that today we would explore outside the Medina again, but this time walk to a 'point of interest' that we had found in the map book. We packed a bag of food and water and set off.

The walk took us past an attractive-looking garden called 'Cyber Gardens', a name that we found intriguing. We went in and found a very attractive garden that provided a sanctuary from the hustle and bustle of Marrakesh street life. But the intriguing aspect of these gardens was that scattered throughout were stand-up 'poles' or 'kiosks' where there was a computer screen and keyboard. These computers were connected to the internet and were free to use by anybody. What an excellent way of enabling anybody, young or old, rich or poor, to be able to access the modern world of online technology. Nick and I were most impressed.

We continued walking towards our destination, walking through some very impressive sections of town, with large, modern hotels and very large, ornate and expensive-looking mansions. We believe that this may have been the part of Marrakesh where the foreign embassies and dignitaries were, which would explain the hotels and fancy houses.

Eventually, we got to our destination, which was a public garden of some sort with an historic reservoir of water. There were two hundred years of history associated with the reservoir, the details of which I don't remember. The more interesting part of the garden for me was that it was in the process of being setup for an exhibition the next day of garden displays made by local primary school children. Some of the displays were already setup, so we stopped by and listened as the school children explained to us in French the details of the theme behind their garden, the work that they had put into building it and what they had learnt through the exercise. As my comprehension of French is virtually nil, I simply judged by the tone of the young voices when I was meant to show surprise, joy and praise. It was wonderful to see the energy and enthusiasm shown by the young students.

As we were walking around, Nick's mobile phone was quite active. He was getting messages from his sister in England and his travel agent, mentioning something about the volcano in Iceland. This still did not really mean much to us, but it did at least shift our focus slightly towards the topic.

After a very pleasant walk we returned to the Medina, spent some time walking around the shops, finally returning to the villa in the late afternoon. While relaxing and preparing to go out again to one of the many restaurants for a tagine and pleasant evening watching the shenanigans in the main square, Nick kept getting messages on his mobile. This was starting to become either annoying or important. We still couldn't decide which one.

As was now the pattern, Nick returned to the villa while I stayed behind to do some emails at the world's slowest internet café. Now it was my turn; Donna was telling me about the volcano in Iceland. So now we were getting it from Nick's contacts on his mobile and from my emails. What the heck did all of this have to do with us?

Tangier or Bust

Friday and the aim today was to do more exploring of the Medina and the souks. A Middle Eastern souk is similar to what we call a market. Importantly, today was the day to buy most of the presents for family and friends that I needed to buy.

While going through the normal morning routine, we learnt from the BBC that the volcano thing was getting more important and was looking like it could affect us. From this, we decided that regardless of what happened, we needed to travel to the airport the next day to at least register our presence and readiness to travel on our scheduled flight. It really was starting to look like it was going to impact us, as they were already talking about flights being cancelled and closing down European air space. I still thought it would all blow over, but we needed to consider our options.

Surprisingly, when we walked up to the main square to do some present shopping, and chose on a whim to walk down a different alleyway, we discovered that there was a whole section of shops, stalls and souks that we hadn't yet even seen. We looked at each other with a shared look of 'Duh'. How could we have missed all of this?

The next couple of hours were taken up by pleasant meandering up one laneway filled with jostling mayhem and down another. We saw stalls selling live chickens and children's shoes, woven carpets and gold jewellery. We saw almost everything that can be bought squeezed into a collection of commotion that stretched the senses. After marvelling at the experience and telling each other, "We're not in Kansas anymore," a few times, clever, huh? We made our way back to the villa and a very pleasant afternoon sitting on the roof drinking wine and eating nuts.

With the now virtually mandatory evening meal of a tagine in another of the restaurants by the square, another pleasant day drew to a close. However, both of us were silently growing more concerned about the volcano and how it could affect us. Tomorrow could be interesting.

We would need all our wits today as this was the day when we would determine if we were returning to England with our booked airline tickets or…? The BBC told us that all was not good and it was definitely looking like no planes were leaving. Nick's almost ceaseless phone messages from England were adding weight to this conclusion. The airspace over Europe was now totally closed due to the risk from volcanic ash and we were hearing that there was travel chaos developing in Europe and England.

After the normal breakfast routine and an update from the BBC, we packed our backpacks with food and water and caught a taxi to the airport. Our intention was to find out what was going on and if our flight was, by some unforeseen magic, actually leaving. If not, then we would need to make alternative plans.

As soon as we arrived we could see that things were not good. For a start, according to the departure boards, the only flights leaving were those heading south to African destinations, or those heading to Middle Eastern places. If it was heading north, it wasn't leaving.

We found the little office for EasyJet to register our presence, only to find that there was already a mumble of 30 hopeful travellers already there doing the same thing. Straight away I didn't feel good about this. We joined the mob and shuffled our feet for the next 15 minutes, waiting our turn at the window. I could soon see that the line wasn't moving. Nick, being English where queuing has become a fine art, was now having a joyful old time chatting with other Brits in the queue. I could feel an upwelling of shrieking frustration forming in by shoes, so I suggested to Nick that he maintain our spot in the line and 'find out what you can' and then took myself off for an explore.

I walked down to the other end of the terminal, only to find that most of the offices and counters were closed. Hmm, I wasn't expecting that. I came across a group of car rental company counters and the spark of a thought suddenly popped up. I kept exploring and finally found a place that sold maps, then paid the most exorbitant price ever for a map of Morocco. It was a good map, but at that price, so it should be. I checked the map to see what further ideas would come from it and discovered that Tangiers, a city still in Morocco, was a short ferry ride from Gibraltar. My spark of an idea was starting to take shape.

As I headed back across the terminal towards Nick, I went over to the car hire counter with the most approachable-looking lady and asked her how much would it cost to hire a car for a one-way trip from Marrakesh to Tangiers. She looked a little surprised and turned to her companion to discuss the request. She told me that it would cost 2000 dirhams. A quick division by seven told me that this was approximately $A280, an amount that I considered acceptable under the circumstances. As I walked back to where Nick was in jovial conversation with his fellow Brits, I was considering my approach. Now being a full grownup, I've finally learnt that you can't just tell someone what they should do, so knew that I had to get Nick 'on board' so that he considered this was a viable option.

I cleared my throat and launched gently into my sales pitch. It started with me whispering in Nick's ear, "This is crazy. We need to find another way to get back to England under our own steam." Nick immediately called on his memories of similar conversations ten or 12 years ago, which ended with us being bogged to the floor in sand for 26 hours, 300 km from civilisation. He looked at me with trepidation in his voice and said, "I'd be happy to wait in Marrakesh to see what happens."

I didn't actually get down on my knees to plead with Nick, but I was prepared to if necessary. Fortunately, after Nick looked at the crowd of people which hadn't moved a millimetre in the past 20 minutes and listened to the voices that were starting to become agitated and frustrated, he realised that we did need to do something. So he asked me what my proposal was. I told him about the car rental and that we could drive to Tangiers. I showed him the map and pointed out the ferry crossing to Gibraltar. His trepidation started to wain as he thought about this and watched the fuss going on around us. Finally, after five minutes of pondering, I had convinced Nick that this was a good option. He was still muttering warnings and caution as we neared the car hire counter. I let him talk to the lady this time as a way to enhance his buy-in, and surprisingly this time the price for the car was down to 1900 dirhams. That was certainly a surprise to me. A minute or two more of decision process and Nick agreed to the plan.

Woohoo! Let the next adventure begin.

Decision made and time to move. Suddenly we had focus and purpose again. Now it was time to get moving and set the extremely loose plan into motion. What am I talking about? We didn't have a plan. All we knew at this moment was that we had rented a car to drive to Tangiers by 3 p.m. the next day. Other than that, all we had was a furry idea that we would catch a ferry across to Gibraltar. That's it as far as a plan went.

We drove the car back to the Medina and parked it so we could walk back to the villa.

STOP! I'm lying.

We started to drive the car back to the Medina, took a wrong turn then got horribly lost. For the next 30 minutes, we drove around the Medina, trying to find a recognisable landmark so we could park the car. Round and round and round we went, getting so caught up in crowded streets full of markets and donkeys that I thought we would never find our way out. This was the START of the new adventure and here we were driving in circles. Oh dear, oh dear, oh dear.

At last and eventually we found the landmark, parked the car and started walking back. But there's no denying that getting so lost so early in our journey was a bit disconcerting. But maybe it was a blessing because it told us not to get cocky and don't take things for granted. We needed to keep our wits about us and keep thinking.

Finally, we came sweeping into the villa full of energy. On the (extended) trip back we'd made a list of what needed to be done, which included going to the ATM to get some travelling cash, packing up all of our stuff, settling the bill with Abdulleila and then going to the supermarket to buy travelling and 'just-in-case' food. This was now exciting as it was the start of a brand-new adventure.

As we were about to leave the villa for the last time and were saying thank you and goodbye to Abdulleila, he asked us where we were going next. We told him that we were going to the supermarket again to get some travelling food and he held out his hand for the car keys. I tried to assure him that we'd be OK, but he virtually insisted that I give him the keys. Nick and I looked at each other because this was a little strange, but we gave him the keys anyway.

As Abdulleila was driving us towards the supermarket we were expecting to go to, I was more than a little curious when he went sailing past it and just kept going. I snuck a glance at Nick sitting in the back seat and we both shrugged our shoulders. Abdulleila's English wasn't very good, plus he was a very shy fellow, so he doesn't talk much. We were now travelling through Marrakesh past the supermarket and heading for… well… we didn't know.

Fifteen minutes later, Abdulleila pulled into the car park of a huge and modern supermarket. He knew that we were going to need a wider range of supplies than the first supermarket stocked, so simply took us to this huge one. I'd love to know what thoughts were going through his mind as he silently guided us on our way. Then again, maybe it's better that I don't. Not only was this supermarket perfect, but it was located on the highway we needed to take to leave Marrakesh and head towards Casablanca. More perfect.

Now we said our final farewell to Abdulleila and gave him money for the taxi fare back to his villa. This was yet another example of how friendly and helpful Moroccan people are. After 20 minutes of shopping for breakfast food—milk, cheese, you know, stuff, we were finally on our way. Tangiers, here we come! It was 4 o'clock in the afternoon.

When we picked the car up from the renters, it had about a half a tank of fuel, and we had no idea what the conditions were like on the highway for fuel between Marrakesh and Tangiers, a distance of almost 600 km. So it was important for us to fill the tank before getting too far from Marrakesh.

Not far along the highway, we found a service station that looked clean and legitimate, so pulled in to fill up. As we drove in, one of the pump attendants jumped up to serve us. He motioned to a pump where he started to put the nozzle into the tank. Surprisingly, it didn't go in, so he motioned for us to move forward to the next pump. That nozzle didn't go in either and I started to consider that things often don't work properly in the Middle East as I moved forward to another pump. With some persuasion, the young fellow was able to get this one in and proceeded to fill the tank.

As usual, we paid for the fuel, got back in the car and started it up. Immediately an older fellow came rushing over and started urgently saying something to me with a raised voice. I had no idea what the problem was and said that I didn't understand what he was saying. Then he did something that both Nick and I found amazing; he reached in through the open window and turned the engine off. I was gobsmacked. I told him that everything was working OK and started the engine again to show him. He rolled his eyes, reached in and turned the engine off again and then took the keys out of the ignition and put them in his pocket.

Now let me do a word sketch of this scene. We are on the outskirts of Marrakesh in Morocco buying fuel before driving 600 km through the night. Nobody speaks English and the older Arabic-speaking fellow has just confiscated our car keys. What would you be thinking?

He indicated for us to get out of the car, then in a very agitated voice he told the young pump attendant to help him push the car over to the workshop. I was starting to get a germ of an idea. We helped to push the car and another fellow came out of the shop and helped as well. As we parked the car in the workshop, I asked this new fellow, who understood some English, if my understanding was correct.

"Had the car just been filled with diesel instead of petrol?"

"Yes," he said. Now it all made sense, but my heart sank to my boots.

This can't be good.

For the next half hour, they worked on the car, while Nick and I were thinking about what we may need to do to save the situation. The basic practicality they used was surprising to me, a person who knows very little about things mechanical. The older fellow got an air hose used to pump up tyres, and wrapped a rag around it. Then he pushed this into the fuel inlet of the petrol tank so it was jammed in. Then he had another piece of tube which he pushed into the tank, with the loose end hanging out and into an empty container. When he let the air go into the tank, the fuel came out of the loose pipe and into the container. Brilliant!

It took around 20 minutes for them to be satisfied that they had all of the diesel out, then they pushed the car back out to the pumps and filled the tank again, this time with petrol. The older fellow indicated for me to start the car and give the accelerator a good pump. All seemed good so far. Then he indicated for me to drive it around the concourse of the station, giving it a good ol' revving as I went. All seemed good.

Phew! It appeared that the situation had been saved by the application of basic mechanical skill and good old common sense. I shook the older fellows hand and thanked him, then offered him some money to compensate for all of the fuel that had been wasted. He looked at me like I was an idiot, said something that was likely to be related to it being their fault and then waved us on our way.

We had left the villa less than two hours ago. This was going to be an interesting journey.

A few kilometres down the highway which, by the way, was a brilliant piece of modern freeway, we came to a long, gradual uphill section. The car, which only had a 1.2-litre motor, started to struggle and lose speed as it climbed. I had the accelerator flat to the floor and it was still losing speed. Before we got to the top it started to miss fire; this was not feeling good. We spluttered gradually to the top of the hill and over the top, where the motor started to run smoothly again. Nick and I were both holding our breath as we willed the car on. Then, with a final cough, it cleared its throat and all was good from that point on. All traces of diesel were now gone.

We drove along enjoying the scenery for the next hour or so until it was time for my injection. I've learnt over the years that when in a country where it's unlikely that the police speak English, it's best not to have my injection in a place that is in view of the public. So we pulled off the main highway and found a secluded spot up a side road. This gave us an opportunity to drive through a small village, where we stopped in the hope of buying some dinner.

While struggling through our enquiry as to whether the chosen place of nutrition was able to provide us with a tagine, a local fellow who surprisingly could speak English, asked me if I could give him some money so he could fix his truck. When I politely declined his kind offer to let me help him financially he, while remaining quite polite, reminded me that I was from 'the west' and was therefore rich. So helping him to fix his truck wouldn't be much of an issue for me. I attempted to clarify for him that not all westerners were rich and that I didn't have much money. Being obviously more worldly that I, he could not be convinced that I uttered the truth. So this interaction, combined with the news that the café did not serve tagines, meant that it was best for us to leave the village and re-join the highway to Tangiers.

We swapped drivers and kept driving into the night. Suddenly Nick slammed on the brakes, briefly putting the car into a skid. Then he swung into the right lane and rocketed past a small truck that was stopped in the middle lane without any lights showing at all. Phew! That was close.

At one point at about 10 o'clock, we stopped at a 24-hour truck stop to have a cup of coffee and a rest from the road. I was checking out the hugely expensive map that I'd bought at the airport and wondered why on the map 'Morocco' in

Arabic was called *'Marob'*. I asked the young fellow behind the counter why this was so and he smiled and shrugged his shoulders. He told us in reasonable English that in Arabic, their country is called *'Maroc'*, but in writing, it is spelled *'Marob'*. He said that he didn't know why this was so.

The highway continued on past Casablanca, where there was a lot of road work being done and the travelling was slow. Then we continued north towards Tangiers until eventually, after a very interesting day of ups and downs, we needed to stop for a sleep. So we pulled off onto a side road, found a spot with a reasonable amount of privacy and set ourselves up for the night.

Now don't forget that we were in a 1.2 litre car with a back seat covered with bags of food and water. There was not a lot of room in this car to stretch out and get comfortable, so this ended up being the most uncomfortable night I have ever spent. It was even more uncomfortable than the night I spent on a rock at Wilsons Prom during my training for this whole adventure. That was luxury compared to what we endured during this night in the car.

The Train in Spain

Sunday—the 18th of April—and the morning was finally here. As soon as there was enough light, I had my morning jabs and breakfast and we prepared to continue on to Tangiers. We had no idea where we would be by the end of the day, but we had to keep moving forward.

Tangiers held a certain fascination for me because it featured in one of the passages from the third Jason Bourne movie. After arriving there at about 11 o'clock, I found that it wasn't like it was in the movie. Surprise, surprise! Tangiers is a reasonably modern city with an obvious strong Portuguese influence in its architecture. We drove straight to the ferry port to find out about the ferry across to Gibraltar, but there was so much fuss going on and people talking in loud voices that it was difficult to learn anything. It also appeared that very few people spoke English, so it all became a bit of a guessing game really.

Nick managed to learn where and how to buy some tickets on the ferry, so we did finally get some. But we also learnt that there was only one ferry to Gibraltar per week, and it just so happened to be today. Now I'm not going to put my hand on my heart and say that this was fact, but it certainly did seem to be a fact. Most of the ferries travelled to other cities further along the coast of Spain with only one travelling to Gibraltar. I found this odd, but it didn't really matter. We now had tickets for the ferry that left in the afternoon.

As we had a few hours until departure time, we drove the car back to the airport to return it to the car hire company. All went well there, but we had another interesting encounter. The car hire fellow asked how we were returning to the ferry port and we told him that we would just catch a taxi, indicating towards the taxis out in the car park area. At this, the fellow urgently stressed that we must not take one of the small taxis, only the big ones. We acknowledged the warning but he stressed it again. He said, "We must not, OK?" We agreed again, thanked him for his help and left. To this day, we don't really know why he was so insistent, so we can only guess that it was either to do with getting cheated in the little taxis OR that they routinely carry multiple fares and we could end up paying way too much or not even getting to our destination. Who knows? But we took one of the large taxis, which was a Mercedes just like you see in the Jason Bourne movie, and had a very pleasant, but interesting, trip back to the port.

Interesting? We had now ourselves travelled to the airport from the port area, so had some experience with how to get there. Our driver, who was a lovely older fellow, went a completely different way. It didn't matter as far as the fare was concerned because it was a set fare, but we again wondered briefly if we were being taken to our destination. It seemed that we did a sightseeing tour of Tangiers, seeing some wonderful Portuguese houses and architecture along the way. I was just starting to wonder if we would ever get there when the driver pulled over and said we were there. He unloaded our bags, we shook hands and said thank you, gave him a small tip then wondered where we were. He pointed down the hill and waved goodbye. Hopefully, we dragged our bags around the corner and there was the port right in front of us.

Mid-afternoon and we were in the departure area for the ferry. We really had very little idea of exactly where it left from or when, as there were ferries regularly arriving and departing for various spots in Spain or further along the North African coast. The best I can say is that the organising of the ferry departure process was ramshackle at best. At one stage, someone said the Gibraltar ferry was about to leave and we had better hurry, so we grabbed our various bags and rushed off, concerned that we would miss the once-a-week ferry. But after a few minutes in the wheezing line, we discovered that this ferry went to a different city in Spain. I was furious about this confusion that had been pressed onto us. We went back to the departure lounge to wait for the proper ferry. The crazy thing is that there wasn't a board in the lounge showing which ferries were leaving or from which berth. There was no indication at all. So it was purely guess work, gossip and panic that kept people moving towards their correct ferries.

Even when our ferry was boarding, we all lined up for over an hour waiting to get on board. When everyone was finally on board and the ferry finally underway, we were 45 minutes behind schedule.

But what a wonderful trip. Firstly the adventurer in me was excited to be on a boat crossing 'The Straights of Gibraltar' (Isn't that exciting for you?) travelling between Africa and Europe, going past all of the freighter traffic entering into the Mediterranean. Secondly, we watched the dolphins playing in the bow wave of another ferry as we went past. This went on for ten minutes, so we saw lots of dolphins as they came diving out and ahead of the ferry. Thirdly, Nick bought a couple of small bottles of wine for the trip, which lasted only 45 minutes. All together it was a great crossing. I have to admit that I almost lost my composure as the ferry was docking. It slowly turned around, so it was facing out again for the return journey and in doing so, The Rock slowly came into our field of view. There it was, THE ROCK OF GIBRALTAR. What a fantastic sight! And as we stepped off the ferry, we were in Europe.

Once through customs, which was an easy exercise because Nick is British and I'm Commonwealth, we set off walking towards La Linea, which is the first town on the Spanish side of the border. Our loose plan was that we were going to catch a train or a coach the next day, heading for Somewhere Else, so it was best for us to go to La Linea. One thing that I found amazing was that to walk from Gibraltar to Spain, you have to walk across the runway of Gibraltar airport. I couldn't believe it; they even have pedestrian traffic lights so you don't get hit by a plane. Cool, huh?

By now, it was raining lightly but not enough to be of any concern. But it did add emphasis to finding a hotel room for the night. We bumped into another Brit who was also walking down the almost deserted street and he told us that there was a hotel up the road on our left. So we headed there, found the hotel and booked in for the night. It was now a quarter past ten, it was raining lightly and getting cold. It was the end of the day.

Monday and the aim today was to be closer to the Lakes District in England than we were in the morning. While Nick had breakfast, I went for a walk around the local streets. In doing so, I found the short cut to the bus station, which was only 500 m from the hotel. So when our breakfast and morning ablutions were complete, we booked out of the hotel and dragged our bags to the bus station.

In Spain, the understanding of English is very close to poor, so making ourselves understood was to be a chore for the next few days. We were finally able to learn that there 'maybe' a train that left from Algeciras, a small city only about 10km away. We waited 15 minutes for the local bus then climbed aboard and paid. I was surprised at how cheap the fare was, being only about 2.5 Euro for each of us. As we were about to sit down a funny thing happened. A local fellow who had a good understanding of English told us that he had closed the door to the luggage compartment under the bus.

Oh yes, I thought. *Uh huh.* The full meaning of his comment was lost on Nick and me. So he kindly expanded and gave us a lesson in Spanish customs. It turns out that while in Spain, it is expected that you do almost everything for yourself. This included putting your own bag in the luggage compartment and then closing the door to the compartment. Apparently the next person then must open the door, put their bag in then close the door again. We were also to find out later in the day that the checkout chicks and guys at a supermarket do not put your groceries in bags as they do in Australia. Nope, they grab some plastic bags and dump them on top of your forlorn groceries. You must then scramble to get them in the bags before the next person gets all bent out of shape because you're in the way. Travelling can be so much fun as you learn these little things.

The trip to Algeciras was only short and delivered us to the main bus terminal, which is only a short walk to the main train terminal. We hurried across the road to the trains with the idea being to get tickets on the next train to Madrid, only to learn that the trains don't run between Algeciras and Madrid. They will in a month but not now, because they're still working on the new or upgraded train line.

Oh.

We asked the fellow behind the glass what our options were, which involved lots of waving of hands as his English wasn't much better than our Spanish. His advice was to go back to the bus terminal and catch a coach to Malaga, which is a tourist town popular with British tourists, about 150 km up the coast. There was a train for Madrid leaving from there. So now it was back to the bus terminal to buy tickets, which were again relatively cheap, to Malaga on a coach that left not long after. Even though we were zigzagging a little, the timing was working out OK.

The trip to Malaga took us along a section of the Spanish coast that surprisingly put Nick in a bad mood. I'd never been to Spain before but living in England, Nick had been here a number of times. Apparently Malaga is the centre of the 'British invasion' of Spain and because of them the countryside is being decimated so they can build kilometre after kilometre of bland, characterless holiday apartments, with British pubs and British Fish 'n Chip shops every 200 m. Nick hated what was happening to a piece of coastline that used to be so beautiful.

After arriving in Malaga and briefly casting around looking for the train station, we finally found it. It's a large station with the ticket office at one end of a big, brand-new shopping centre, the whole building surrounded by construction work, which is why it was hard to find. We joined the queue for tickets and started sharing travel stories with our fellow queue waiters. This was where we started to find an ever growing group of stranded travellers and their various stories of midnight journeys. The volcano had created havoc in Europe and it seemed that half the world was now dragging suitcases along behind them.

As the line slowly shrank and we got closer to the ticket booth, we began to overhear conversations that were saying that there were no available seats to Paris. Our general idea had been that we would catch a train to Paris, make our way to Calais and then get a ferry from there to England. But that was now seeming unlikely at best.

When it was finally our turn, Nick used his meagre Spanish to talk to the very patient and helpful fellow, who confirmed that all seats from Madrid to Paris were fully booked. We could, if we wanted to, take a train from Madrid to Barcelona on the 'chance' that there were seats available from Barcelona to Paris, but he couldn't guarantee there would be. I was OK with taking that option but Nick thought it was silly to be effectively travelling backwards to maybe get a seat. So he asked the very patient fellow for other alternatives. He said that another way would be to travel to Madrid, then catch a train from there to Santander on the north coast of Spain. An overnight ferry left from Santander, bound for Plymouth in England. Suddenly this appeared to be the best option, as at least we were closer to England, so we bought two tickets.

As the train didn't leave for about an hour and a half, we had time to relax, have a cup of coffee and for me to find a supermarket. I asked somebody where I could find one and they told me that there was one in another shopping centre a kilometre away. So I left Nick to relax with a coffee while I took off to get my new bag of travelling food.

I found the supermarket, which was huge, and left my backpack with the bag guard, in a locker by the exit. Off I went to get my required food, such as some fruit, cheese, water, etc. and then went to the checkout. This is where I experienced the Spanish checkout process for the first time. They have a stick in the place where they push your groceries down after pricing them. When she has finished, the girl grabs just enough plastic bags, minus one, and dumps them on top of your groceries. She then slides the stick across to allow her to push down the groceries for the next customer, leaving you to get your groceries packed into the too few bags as quickly as you can. At first, I had no idea what I was supposed to do, then realised, so started packing the bags. I ran out of bags before I'd run out of groceries, so the nice lady beside me, the other customer, gave me another one. She didn't smile or say a word—just handed over the extra bag.

After finishing my shopping, I grabbed my bags and headed back to the station, where Nick was sitting in the café still with his coffee. We were sitting there relaxing before our train trip when, with less than half an hour to go before the train left, I suddenly realised that my backpack was missing! What the—?!! I looked around and couldn't see it. I thought back over the past ten minutes and realised that there were times over the last ten minutes when I hadn't had my eyes on my bags, so assumed immediately that my backpack had been picked up by someone walking past. I told Nick it was missing so we could share the feeling of panic. We went over what my backpack contained, to see if there was something critical in there and determined that there wasn't. But still, it was MY backpack which I had used in the Sahara and I DIDN'T WANT TO LOSE IT! I was very much not happy.

Furious, I went to the toilet. Suddenly, at a rather inopportune moment, I realised what had happened. My backpack was still back at the supermarket in the security locker. I'd been so intrigued by the whole shopping bag packing routine at the checkout that I had entirely forgotten to pick up my backpack.

I came running back to the café, where Nick was still looking mighty concerned, and told him I knew where it was and that I'd be back in time for the train. Then I took off and ran back to the supermarket, got my backpack from the security fellow and ran back to the station. We rushed off to the train and got there with five minutes to spare. Phew, what a drama.

We were now entering a whole different world. This was the world of high-tech and very expensive to build, very high speed trains. Wow, do we need these trains in Australia! On the way from Malaga to Madrid we hit 300 kph. For anyone in a non-metric country, this equals more than 180 mph. And it was as smooth as glass. The countryside was beautiful as it swept past, usually at more than 200kph. In France, there are a lot of vineyards; in Spain there are a lot of olive groves. The trip from Malaga to Madrid took only around three hours.

As our train to Santander the next day was leaving at 6:50 a.m. from a different station to that which we pulled in to, common sense dictated that we needed to travel to the next station and find a hotel room near there. That would make it much easier to get to the train so early in the morning. After leaving the station, we caught a taxi and, after driving through a chunk of Madrid, were soon at the second station.

Fortunately, there was a hotel right there at the station, so we quickly went in to get a room. It was becoming less of a surprise for us now to see that there was already a short line of people booking in, so we just silently hoped that there was a still a room. And there was.

We settled in to our new room then, as I didn't need to get a bag of food tonight, we went down to the station to see where we had to go in the morning. While exploring the food shops that were open, and looking amazed at how many families were preparing to bed down for the night in the station forecourt, we came across a car hire place. Suddenly this started a whole new discussion between Nick and me. The car hire place wasn't open, but we started discussing the possibility of hiring a car the next morning and driving to France and the ferries. We convinced ourselves so readily that this was a workable option that I even went to the train ticket office to see if I could cash in our tickets to Santander. Annoyingly, and fortunately, the girl on the other side of the counter claimed to have no English at all, and even less patience with whatever I was trying to tell her. So I cracked it and stormed off in a hissy fit, waving the tickets over my shoulder and telling her that she could have had them back in order to sell them to somebody else. I know, I know; she was shaking in her boots. We stomped back to our room, well, I stomped and Nick walked, and settled down for the night.

While preparing for sleep, we tuned the TV into BBC and listened to the latest news. With regard to the volcano disruption, which was still the main story, this included an item about rumours that car hire places were starting to charge a fortune to hire cars and another item about the ferries from

Calais being thoroughly and completely booked out for the next week.

Oh… we weren't expecting that. Oh… ummmm, maybe we needed to rethink this. What do we have? We have booked tickets to Santander on a train that leaves from just downstairs. What don't we have? We don't have any idea if we really can get a car, how much it will cost, even if they will let us drive it to France. We also don't know if we can get on a ferry if we get to Calais. There was one other interesting story on the BEEB, and that was that a British Navy ship was at Santander to pick up stranded Brits and take them back to Blighty.

At this, we again changed our minds. We clutched our train tickets lovingly to our hearts and silently thanked the girl downstairs for not helping us.

In the Navy—Almost

Early on Tuesday morning, we were down stairs at the station, ready for the train to leave. The news on the TV had continued to tell us that there was growing concern that car hire companics were taking unfair advantage of the crisis and that the ferries all along the French coast were booked out for a week. So we were glad that we were waiting for the train to leave for new fields.

As we were coming to expect, the train left precisely on time. My brief experience with the Spanish railways is that they are brilliant, with modern clean trains, good service and uncanny timeliness.

The countryside between Madrid and Santander was hillier than the previous day, as there are a line of mountains that run across the northern coast of Spain. We needed to cross these mountains before we got to Santander, so the maximum speed we reached on the whole trip was, when compared to the previous day, a rather ambling 230 kph. I have to say that the Spanish countryside is beautiful and I can strongly recommend a train holiday.

When we arrived in Santander, Nick and I quickly made our way downhill from the train station. We had no idea where we were going but knew that the port had to be downhill from the station. It wasn't long before we saw the ocean, so knew we were heading in the right direction.

As we scampered along with as much dignity as we could maintain, we came to realise that we were leading roughly 20 other desperate-looking tourists with bags as we all rushed hopefully towards the navy ship. Now you need to remember that none of us actually knew that the ship was still here. Not only that but none of us knew where on Earth the ship was docked. It could have been kilometres up the coast for all we knew, as we hurried along looking like the Keystone Kops.

But it wasn't; it was right there in front of us in all its glory as we turned the corner. There was a huge, grey, very impressive-looking navy ship, complete with guns and all sorts of navy stuff, and it was right here in the heart of Santander. So the Keystone Kops, with us in the lead, stepped up the dignified pace a notch.

We all raced for the gate in the fence where there were guards standing. As we got there they were saying something in an unhopeful sounding voice. Everyone behind us started shouting their questions together as desperation to get home replaced dignity, so I concentrated intently on what the guards were saying. For those who were listening, which added up to Nick and me, we soon learnt that this ship wasn't taking any of us anywhere.

I turned to Nick and said, "This isn't going to work. We need to get to the ferry terminal."

Nick said, "I agree. The ferry terminal is up this way; I saw it as we came down."

So Nick and I turned on our heels and, as rapidly as we could without actually breaking into a run, rushed up the port area for 200m to the ferry terminal office, with our bags bouncing joyfully behind us on their tiny little wheels. The Keystone Kops soon came to the same realisation as we had, but now they didn't need to decide which way to go; they simply followed us, so we were losing our 'advantage'. (Can you feel the desperation in the air? So could we.) We rushed into the ferry office, took two seconds to do a reconnoitre and then rushed to the end of the line waiting to buy tickets. We were the first of the recent train arrivals to make it to the ferry line. Mwahahahaaaa!

This line was moving slowly but steadily. The ladies behind the desk were looking amazingly calm considering they were dealing with a bunch of desperate tourists ready to sell their firstborn if the sale secured a spot on The Ferry. Nick and I kept our ears peeled (I'm writing this story, so I'll mix metaphors if I want to) so we could learn everything to be learnt. And what we learnt was that indeed there was a ferry on Thursday that was travelling to Plymouth in England. However, all seats and cabins were fully booked but the ferry operators were prepared to let in a certain number of extra passengers who would need to sleep where ever they could find a spot.

The line of people was beginning to take on a party atmosphere as everyone exchanged their volcano stories. So 'n so had travelled from Somewhere on Such 'n such bus to be here. Oh the drama, oh the cost! But they were all struck dumb when Nick and I told them our story. The usual response we got was a pause and then a tentative: "Really? You've come cross-country from Marrakesh?"

Finally, it was our turn to buy tickets. I was nervously hopeful as we took our spot at the desk. The nice lady, who spoke very good English, explained the situation to us then sold us two tickets. I was thrilled to finally have ferry tickets to England for the day after next so, as we walked back past the line of waiting people, I did a little happy dance, waving my tickets in the air.

I found out two days later that the people immediately behind us in the queue were the last to get tickets for the Thursday ferry as it was then full. Oops!

Now the next race was on. Sure, we had tickets for the ferry, but we still didn't have a room for the night. We stepped outside the ferry office and looked around. There, across the road was a good-looking hotel, the Hotel Bahia. Because we were still in front of the Keystone Kops, we still considered that we needed to hurry, so with hardly a word Nick and I dragged our bags across the road to the hotel and booked in for two nights. And a lovely hotel it was too.

Now was the first chance since leaving Marrakesh for us to be able to simply relax. We didn't have any commitments from now, which was 2 o'clock in the afternoon, until 1 o'clock Thursday afternoon when the ferry was loading. So we lounged around for a bit, watching the BBC to keep up with the news. From our window, we were able to watch the navy ship leave. It was very impressive but also rather galling because, for a brief moment, it had seemed that we may have been able to come swanning back into England in style, but that moment had soon passed. Reality had smacked us as we, and the rest of the Keystone Kops, had been left on the dock. And now we could stand and watch as it slowly pulled out and left us all behind.

The rest of the afternoon was taken up with doing emails, going to the supermarket for the bags of emergency food, exploring the beautiful city of Santander and amazing at the architecture. Being from Oz, I've never heard of The Bank of Santander, but apparently in Europe it is an important bank. Well guess where the beautiful head office is? That's right, Santander. It was just behind the hotel we were in.

Exploring a new city is one of the joys of travelling. It is wonderful to be wandering slowly down a street then suddenly come across a building that has a market inside selling all sorts of exotic salamis and cheeses. There were all sorts of cafes, bars and restaurants. There was too much to take in in one afternoon. Next to the hotel was a lovely garden area with a café and a children's play area. In the play area was a beautiful and classic carousal, with the lights and the bobbing horses. Doting parents could sit at the outdoor café drinking coffee and eating cakes while the children went round and round on the carousal. To be honest, I was struggling to comprehend how Spain could be caught up in the deep financial problems sweeping through Europe. It certainly didn't look like it from our perspective as we explored this prosperous-looking city.

That night we wandered off looking for a café or restaurant to have dinner. Because we were in Spain, Nick had a desire to have a typically Spanish dish called *paella*, which we came to learn is pronounced *paaya*. Plus he considered that there was a good chance that paella would be gluten-free, which meant that I could also have it for dinner.

We walked up the road checking out the various cafes and restaurants, finally settling on one that looked like it would fit the bill, Café Te. The main waitress was a small lady who was full of life, laughing and cajoling customers in a loud voice. When it came time for us to order, it was fun as we decided with her whether the paella in the picture was gluten free. Her

English was, well, nil and my Spanish was, well, virtually nil. However, Nick, with his combination of reasonable French and slight Spanish was able to translate and understand much of what she was describing. So between us we decided that the *paella* in the picture was worth the small risk for me. Fortunately, this was another example of how the Spanish are well aware of gluten-free, so our charming waitress knew why it was important for me to know what was in the dish. It was all good fun deciding all of this, with lots of laughing and joking.

The evening went on with her yelling incomprehensible jokes in our direction and, after a little more of the red grape juice, us yelling back at her with lots of laughing. But finally, it was time to leave and for us to wander back to the hotel. A quick catch-up of the latest news on the Beeb and we called the day over.

The next day, Wednesday, was a rest day as we waited for the ferry. Of course we kept a close eye on the volcano updates, which were going from bad to worse. We heard that now the recriminations had started, with airlines and others saying that the governments had over reacted by closing down the airspace. I was in two minds; firstly I don't like the way western governments are rapidly becoming nanny states, but then I don't relish the idea of falling out of the sky because the engines of the plane got clogged. I think sometimes there are situations where there simply isn't an easy option.

So Nick and I pushed all of that to the back of our mind and set out to explore Santander. I won't bore you with the details, so I'll just say that Santander is a city that would be a good addition to any travel schedule in Spain. It's an attractive, clean city with beautiful architecture and great restaurants.

We did take the opportunity to call into a number of cafés throughout the day to sit and watch the people. One observation is that the Spanish are yet to embrace the idea of giving up cigarettes. It seems that every second person has a cigarette in their mouth, as it used to be at home. Because it has changed so much in Melbourne over the last 20 years, the Spanish reality was a bit surprising.

That night, we returned to the same café as the previous night to have the meal that I knew was good for me. Aside from the food, it was good fun there. I have to be honest and tell you that this night we were a little more free 'n easy with the grape juice and were again the last to leave before they closed the doors.

This was a quiet day of rest, cafés and exploring.

Finally it was the day when, all going well, we were heading back to England. The morning went as normal, with no great surprises. The Beeb was still telling us about the throngs of stranded travellers and were focussing particularly on the main train station in Madrid. Apparently, this had become a focal point for tourists coming from all over southern Europe and it was becoming rather chaotic. As we had been there only two days previously, we were again surprisingly pleased that we had managed to stay ahead of the main mob. Call it good planning, thinking outside the square or just dumb luck, we'd had a good dollop of it to get us to northern Spain and a ferry this afternoon.

One of our important tasks was to buy emergency food to get us through that night on the ferry and two train trips once we got to England. So we spent a little bit of time ensuring we had more than enough to get us through.

At last, it was time to book out of the hotel and make our way across the road to the ferry terminal, where we found a substantial line of people already queued up. We joined the queue and waited patiently as more and more people joined after us. The room became full of people and their suitcases. There were families with babies and old people and young people; there were backpackers and businessmen. It seemed as if half the world was on the move.

While waiting for the queue to move, we got talking with those around us and swapping war stories… again. During this enjoyable and intriguing activity, we came to learn that two days before, when we had been buying our tickets, the people further back in the line behind us then had missed out. The next ferry for them wasn't until the following Saturday, that is two days from now. I crouched down a little, remembering back to my little victory dance as we walked past the rest of the line. Oh dear.

Unfortunately, it took at least an hour of queuing before the line even started to move. Then once it did, it took another 45 minutes of slow, slow lava flow before we were finally on the ship.

When we did finally get on board we saw, to our amazement, what a brilliant little ship this was. It looked like it was almost brand-new, with restaurants, a cinema, coffee shops, you name it. We explored merrily for half an hour before finally deciding where we were going to spend the night. People were finding whatever seat they could find, and we chose some in a reasonably quiet area, sharing with a couple of ladies from New Zealand, a husband and wife couple from England, who were nice enough to make a donation to my chosen charity after they finally got home, and a quiet backpacker from South America who mainly kept his own counsel.

Of course, because we were on a ship going across the ocean from Spain to England, I was as excited as a kid. But if you overlook this detail, this was one of the worst night's sleep I have ever had. I simply could not get comfortable and spent much of the night wandering around the ferry, trying not to disturb the lucky people who were sleeping. Some chose to party almost all night in one of the pub areas, but even they eventually quietened down and went to sleep. I know because I was there to see it. It was an awful night's sleep.

Not only could I not get to sleep, but as I was coming back to my seat at one point, walking without my shoes on, I stubbed my toe on a chrome upright that was so polished and shiny that I couldn't see it. I heard a crack and knew then that I'd broken my toe. Sure enough, five weeks later and it's still a little bruised and swollen.

And so the night passed.

Homeward Bound

Friday at last and a beautiful, nautical morning. After a very peaceful morning of sailing, singing, "Yo, ho, ho, and a cup of coffee," the ferry docked at Plymouth around 11:30. After an orderly disembarkation and passport check, we discovered that the British railway people had put on buses to take the passengers to the local train station. I was quite happy about this, as it simplified what would have been a mad rush to catch the train that we were booked on. Nick, on the other hand, was dumb founded, as the train people had thought of a way to actually help us poor wandering travellers as we finally got back to Blighty from our traumatic, volcano induced, meanderings. Since riding across Spain at 300 kph on a modern, sleek train, Nick's opinion of British railways had taken a huge hit. So for a bus to be there waiting was a big surprise for him.

After getting to the station and having a cup of coffee, we boarded the first of two trains needed to get us north to Carlisle. This one took us to Birmingham, where we had to change to another for the final leg.

Even though I was now approaching brain dead after all the travelling, I was never-the-less enthralled to watch the English countryside rush past. There's something about

England that I will never get used to; it was like we were travelling across a postcard. The English countryside is so quaint and beautiful and, coming from Australia, lush and green.

Apart from an extraordinary number of people travelling on the trains, nothing too devastating happened as we travelled north. Nick arranged with his friend that he would pick us up at Penrith, which is the station just before Carlisle. So as we finally disembarked and dragged our bags across to the exit gate, there was Russell with a big grin on his face. Hands were shaken and backs were slapped, before we piled into the car for the exciting 20-minute trip to Nick's home in Cockermouth. Now for those nitty picky people out there in reader land, Nick doesn't actually live in Cockermouth. I have come to learn that he lives in a tiny little village ten minutes' walk from Cockermouth called Papcastle. Regardless, it was all utterly beautiful.

After much to do in Morocco, Gibraltar, Spain and England, Nick was finally home and I could relax for a couple of days. It would still be another four days before I'd be home.

The main activity on Saturday was to go for a serious walk in the hills of the Lakes district. I learnt from Nick and Russell that they're not called hills in the Lakes district, but instead are known as 'Fels'. This is an old Viking word that translates to… hill. So we went walking on a magnificent track that took us from a valley of stunning beauty up into the hills, along some spectacular ridges past patches of snow, then down to a small lake and back to the car. Russell volunteers for the local search'n'rescue group and had some amazing stories to tell of people that they've rescued over the years. This part of the country is more than beautiful; it is also potentially dangerous for wannabe adventurers who don't properly prepare themselves.

That night we walked down to Cockermouth where I was able to see the incredible damage caused by the recent floods. The main street had been two metres under water and the evidence was there to be seen. Many of the shops and other buildings on the main street were boarded up waiting for resurrection. We went to one of Nick and Russell's local pubs for a drink and to meet some of the local characters.

I couldn't get over the feeling that I was walking through a movie set, so different was it to what we have in Oz.

Sunday was a relatively quiet day. We visited with one of Nick's neighbours, a charming older couple of late 80s. He was a veteran of the British army in colonial India, complete with footmen and butler. She was a survivor of the German concentration camps and between them they had many fascinating stories to listen to.

We went for a drive into a different part of the Lakes district to see a conservation project to protect a breeding pair of Osprey. These are hunting birds, very rare in this part of England. Some very dedicated people, including Nick, volunteer to protect the birds and enable visitors to experience this rare event.

Afterwards, on the way back to Cockermouth, we stopped at a country pub for a drink. This is another thing about England that fascinates me; the ceiling in the pub was so low that it felt like it was falling on me. A tall man would be only just under the ceiling. It is all very enchanting.

Finally, we did the ubiquitous trip to a supermarket so I could stock up for my long trip the next day, back to Melbourne. This was the last opportunity I would have to buy my 'just-in-case' and travelling food, so I needed to be careful what I bought. I stocked up on fruit juice, gluten-free energy bars and biscuits.

A roast leg of lamb for dinner and this day was now complete.

Today, my last day in England and the first day of my trip home, started at 5 o'clock. I was booked on to the 6:49 train to London from Carlisle.

Nick, who works in Carlisle, was all dressed up in his suit ready for work as he dropped me off at the station. This was an emotional time for both of us as it had been ten years since we had seen each other and now it was coming to an end. Not only that but we had together just completed an adventure trip the like of which doesn't happen very often, and we had survived the experience. We had begun making loose plans for Donna and myself, Nick and some other friends to recreate this whole experience in four years from now, but for now we needed to say goodbye.

As I was in Melbourne when I left, I was revved up for the upcoming trip. But for Nick, this was the final end of the whole experience. It was an emotional farewell between two friends who have experienced a lot of adventure together. It was Nick with whom I was stuck in The Empty Quarter of Saudi Arabia for 26 hours back in 1999 when our cars got bogged to the floor in the sea of sand. When the train came and I was on board and seated, Nick stayed until the train was out of sight.

It was on this trip to London that I learnt an interesting thing about booking a ticket on British trains. I didn't know it when I booked the ticket, but you can buy a ticket without reserving a seat. Reserving the seat involves an extra charge.

As I didn't understand this when booking the ticket a couple of months previously, before the trip was over I found myself standing in the aisle. The person who had reserved the seat I was using got onto the train and then, in a very English way, politely informed me that they 'thought I may have been in the seat that they had reserved'. By now, I had figured out the way it all worked so vacated the seat without question. I simply found another empty seat and sat there, hoping that this one wasn't also reserved. Fortunately, I was able to sit there undisturbed until we arrived in Euston.

I had arranged to meet Tina at Euston so she could give me the suitcase that I had left at her place. Ken came as well and we said our goodbyes, then Tina kindly drove me to Heathrow. It seemed to take a lot of time to get there, but then I'm clueless about the geography of London.

After saying goodbye to Tina at Heathrow, I was now on my own for the rest of my journey home. As I prefer, I was about three hours early for my flight, which gave me time to calm down, check my baggage and take time having some lunch and generally just taking things easy. At least that's how it was meant to go, but my very first official duty turned that on its head. An interesting journey home had just begun.

As I was going through the baggage scanner that checks all hand luggage before entering the passenger area of the terminal, the scanner operator asked me if I had any containers of liquid in my luggage larger than 100 ml. I had my emergency fruit juice which, in my slightly stressed state of mine, I couldn't remember if it was bigger than 100 ml. I took them out to see and saw that they were 200 ml each. The operator told me that I would need to discard them in the bin as they were too big to go on the plane. I explained to him that

I was diabetic and that these were my emergency source of carbohydrate if I needed it on the plane. Entirely dispassionately, he asked me if I had a letter from my doctor. I told him that yes, I did have a doctor's letter. Then he asked me the most unthinking, uncaring, foolish question I think I have ever been asked in relation to my diabetes. He asked me if the letter stated specifically and clearly that I must take the fruit juice on board because it was my emergency source of carbohydrate. Well of course the letter didn't say that. When I told him that, he said in the same unflinching and unemotional tone of voice that I would need to discard the fruit juice.

I was dumbfounded. As I dumped the fruit juice in the bin, I asked the fellow if there was a doctor on board the plane. He said he didn't know and asked me why. I told him that because I had to dump my fruit juice, "The chances are quite good that I will need the doctor before the flight is finished." The dispassionate, uninterested look in his eye didn't change a jot. The ultimate irony of this transaction will become clearer soon.

After this joy was a relatively calm couple of hours as I whiled away the time waiting for departure. Eventually, we all filed onto the plane as normal and waited to take off. And we waited… and we waited.

Eventually, the captain came over the intercom, telling us in his overly calm captain's voice, "Due to heavy traffic at Heathrow today, we're going to be a little delayed with take-off." Oh, great! I had less than an hour between this flight arriving in Doha and my next flight leaving for Melbourne.

We sat on the tarmac, with me slowly but surely going quietly around the twist, for 50 minutes before the captain told us that we had been cleared for take-off. So before we even left Heathrow we were 50 minutes behind schedule.

The flight itself went OK. Surprisingly, and quite happily I must add, I didn't get poisoned on this leg of the flight, so that left only one more chance for them to try again. I hope they forgot on that leg as well. The flight from London headed east and we had taken off at about 4 p.m., so it wasn't long before the sun went down and we were flying in the dark.

As we descended into Doha, I got everything ready for a mad dash through the terminal to get to my connecting flight. And we've all been in the situation where, just because you're in a hurry, everything else seems to be going slow. Like rushing down the footpath on Collins St, dashing to make the train at Flinders St; you can guarantee that there are hordes of slow moving tourists not only scattered on the footpath, but actually lined up military-style across the footpath, so that you almost have to step out onto the road to get past them. Well, that's how it seemed now.

Finally, they let us off the plane. Once into the tunnel thing, another lady who was trying to make a connection to Hong Kong and myself, started running. I didn't care quite so much now about 'doing an ankle'; I just wanted to get to my flight.

We quickly made it to the line-up for the x-ray baggage check. Doha is a strange terminal because, even though we were simply swapping from one plane to another, and would be in the terminal for only minutes, we still had to put our cabin luggage through the x-ray machine. I couldn't believe it. And to add insult to injury, the line was huge.

The lady from Hong Kong was urging me, almost insisting, that we duck under the tapes and push ourselves to the front of the line. I was caught between a rock and a hard place because my polite Australian sensibilities were telling me to take my position and wait my turn. But as the lady was saying, I would definitely miss my flight. So in a rush of decision, I ducked under the tapes and pushed through the crowd to the front. As you would expect, there were lots of complaints and just a little loud muttering from those already in the queue, but my choices were limited.

I pushed to the front then had a choice of two x-ray machines. As I stood there impatiently, waiting to see which machine would free up first, I could feel the daggers being mentally thrust into my back from those behind me. It was only a matter of time before a meaty hand landed on my shoulder to haul me backwards to the back of the line.

Luckily, the machine in front of me came free, so I rushed forward. The operator of this machine was a large and very serious-looking lady who looked like she'd been doing this job for a long, long time, so when I rushed forward, bleating that my flight was in the process of leaving, she looked entirely disinterested. Of course I was hoping that she would wave me through but no, I had to do the right thing and put my bags through. In hindsight, of course that was totally understandable. But what happened next was just one of life's cruelties.

As I was grabbing my bag and about to rush off for the plane, the operator stopped me and said something about the contents of my bag. I didn't clearly hear what she said, but obviously she wasn't happy about something, so to save time I immediately started tearing my bag open. I think I was mouthing off to her a little bit, but she sat there entirely dispassionately waiting for me to bring out the contents. She again mentioned what it was she wasn't happy about and I was able to pick up something about a knife. I was about to scoff and waffle on about: "How could there be a knife in my luggage? I've just come from Heathrow?" when it hit me like a ton of bricks. While I was at Heathrow and swapping over contents from my cabin luggage, backpack and the suitcase that Tina had brought me, I had accidentally left my Swiss army knife in the plastic bag that it had been in since I'd left Melbourne. My mistake was that at Heathrow, I had unthinkingly put that plastic bag, which contained all of my emergency gear for the Sahara, into my cabin luggage. The only reason for that choice was 'just in case I might need something' during the trip back to Melbourne. At no point did it even occur to me that I had a knife in there. Heathrow either didn't see it or chose to let it through but here at Doha, where I would be for a grand total of five minutes and running the whole time, the lady was making a big deal about it. And before you say it, yes, I know she was correct in what she was saying.

Well, with moments left until the plane left, I simply ripped the knife out of the plastic bag and gave it to her, stuffed the bag and everything else back into my cabin luggage, hurled an ill-chosen and none-too-clever sarcastic remark over my shoulder and grabbed my bag and ran.

With the adrenalin surging and all of my senses screaming along on hyper, I quickly found where I had to go and ran down the stairs to the departure lounge. I was there for only a couple of minutes before the transfer bus came and we all filed on for the short trip to the plane. Everyone in the departure lounge and on the bus seemed so calm and patient. My adrenalin still hadn't stopped surging, so I started to breathe calmly to bring myself back down. Then, of course, I needed to consider that, after the stress and rushing and turmoil of the last 30 minutes, my sugar was soon to drop. As I have said many times previously in this story, type 1 diabetes never ever lets you forget, so as well as making sure I had my required papers and documents available and safe, and my bag with me, and was following instructions from the various airline people, I also had to eat some of my 'just-in-case' food that I still carried in my pockets.

Finally, I was on the plane. It was only 15 or 20 minutes since my London flight had pulled into the docking bay and now I was sitting on my final flight to Melbourne. At last, I could begin to relax.

But as with almost every step of this fantastic voyage, the surprises were not yet over. As we sat on the tarmac, still in the docking bay, with me slowly calming down and settling in the for the 12- or 13-hour flight, the plane jolted slightly as it began to pull out, then stopped. No big deal. So far that didn't even raise any interest. As we waited and the seconds, then the minutes ticked by, I realised that this had now been elevated to the abnormal bucket.

After a few minutes, the captain came over the intercom and informed us, in his calm captain voice that, while pushing us out of our docking bay the push truck, you know, the squat little tractor vehicles with the huge wheels had, wait for it, "bent the push rod. I've never known this to happen before, so you're the lucky first."

He then went on to tell us that they were bringing a replacement push rod and it would take about 45 minutes.

I couldn't believe it. It didn't really matter in the big scheme of things, because I didn't have any ongoing flights to catch, but after five weeks of uproar I was keen on getting home to Melbourne. And now we were sitting in the departure bay of Doha airport in Qatar at midnight, waiting for a pushrod thingy that never breaks to be replaced, because it had broken. That sort of summed up my whole trip.

I smiled.

The rest of the flight went according to plan. I didn't get poisoned, which came as a relief. The food situation passed without too much hassle. I got restless, as I'm apt to do on long flights, and walked up and down the aisle like a drifting ghost. Everybody else was snoring away peacefully while I paced. An interesting thing about the flight, which I touched on earlier, was that we were heading east. The plane took off from Doha at about 1 o'clock in the morning and went for 12 or 13 hours. You would think that we would land in Melbourne in the early afternoon and it would be broad daylight. But because we were heading east and going against the direction of the sun, the daylight outside the window lasted for only a short number of hours and then it was again night. It was 10 o'clock at night when we landed in Melbourne, so in one flight we'd gone from night to day to night. That was a bit weird.

There was only one small interesting thing happening at the airport. The passport check, baggage collection and customs checks all went as smoothly as you could hope for. The interesting little thing was that Channel 7, a local TV station, had signs up saying that they were recording an episode of Border Security at the airport that night. That wasn't a big deal, but did fit in with the general pattern of the whole trip. Nothing was simple and nothing was normal.

Finally outside in the public area and there was the family waiting for me. Hugs and kisses from all and life was good.

My journey was over. 2014, here I come.